Troubled Times

Troubled Times

A Journey of Survival and Redemption Beyond the Convent Walls
2024

— — ———————————— — —

Frances Reilly

2024

Author of Suffer the Little Children / The Orphanage

Dedication

Aiden,

I never saw him again after he was interned,
but I've often thought of him.

Acknowledgements

To Robert Smith, my agent and advocate, whose dedication and expertise were instrumental in bringing my debut book, "Suffer the Little Children," to fruition. Your feedback on this manuscript is much appreciated. I am grateful for your efforts in securing the necessary permissions, including the waiver from my ex-husband, George, which allowed me to share my story.

To my son, Darren Young, your meticulous reviews of the manuscript were invaluable.

To my youngest son, Chris Young, whose work, and support were indispensable throughout this journey. I am deeply grateful for your dedication and support. Without you, this project would not be finished.

To Keven Young, the father of my two youngest sons, for his support and encouragement.

Thank you to all those who have supported me along the way, whether through words of encouragement, practical assistance, or being there when I needed a shoulder to lean on. Thank you.

Contents

Prologue .... - 1 -

My New Life .... - 3 -

Missing Molly ....- 18 -

Freedom.. - 28 -

Crazy About Bruce Lee .... - 49 -

Unexpected News .... - 56 -

The Wedding .... - 65 -

Bloody Sunday .... - 78 -

Revelations .... - 84 -

Moving in Day .... - 92 -

My Beautiful Daughter ....- 105 -

A Bomb in the Army Camp............................ - 117 -

A Home of Our Own ....- 124 -

A Welcome Visitor ....- 128 -

The Punch Bag...- 136 -

Dog food pie.. - 140 -

The Explosion ....- 144 -

The Last Rights..- 150 -

Internment ....- 158 -

The Hotel...- 163 -

Epilogue... - 177 -

Prologue

After the heartwarming reception to my debut book, 'Suffer the Little Children,' I felt compelled to pen this sequel. The original has been reimagined with a fresh cover and rebranded as "The Orphanage." I extend my gratitude to Orion Publishers for forwarding the touching acknowledgement letters from readers worldwide, many of whom expressed a keen interest in the events following my departure from the convent. To those who shared their thoughts with me, I offer my sincere thanks; your words have deeply touched me.

Growing up alongside two of my sisters in the Nazareth House convent in Belfast, under the harsh rule of Catholic nuns, conditions were terrible: we were deprived of the most basic necessities and suffered horrendous abuse.

This book has been long overdue due to the demands of my bustling family life. Delving into the most painful chapters of my past required time and resolve. Although this project was initiated years ago, I'm gratified to have finally brought it to fruition. The title, "Troubled Times," was selected to reflect the tumultuous period of my life against the backdrop of the Troubles in Northern Ireland. Out of respect for old acquaintances, many of whom have faded from my life, I have altered most names within this narrative.

I hope my narrative sheds light on the struggles faced by too many children, like myself, thrust into the world ill-prepared and lacking essential support and self-worth. At the tender age of fifteen, I left the convent and confronted the daunting task of survival devoid of love or guidance.

I have come to believe that much of what happened to me after leaving the convent was inevitable. My life there, fraught with trauma, and devoid of love, left me ill-equipped to navigate the complexities of the world. While my constant mistreatment, by the nuns, normalised such behaviour. It was not until I witnessed the effect this behaviour had on those I loved that I realised how abnormal and destructive it was. Regrettably, countless others have endured similar ordeals and continue to grapple with their struggle.

One positive gesture from my former husband was his agreement to sign a waiver affirming his misconduct and my innocence during our time together. While I'm grateful for this, I cannot condone his reprehensible actions detailed in these pages.

Although forgiveness remains elusive, I have found solace in the peace and happiness of my present life, surrounded by a supportive circle of friends and family.

My New Life

Northern Ireland 1969

I watched as the convent gates gradually receded into the distance until they were nothing but a faint memory in the rearview mirror. Relief washed over me, mingled with a profound sense of freedom. My mind buzzed with visions of the road ahead, filled with endless possibilities. Whatever awaited me beyond those gates, it had to be an improvement on the years of suffering endured under the strict rule of the nuns.

I shuddered at the thought of my youngest sister, Sinead, still confined within those walls. The mere idea of her remaining behind was paralysing. I longed for her to be by my side, embarking on this journey of freedom together. Promising that I would visit her as soon as possible, I vowed to bring her sweets and cigarettes as many visitors did, despite the risk of being caught and temporarily banned from visiting.

As I settled into my seat, I tried to release the stress of convent life. Watching the fields of sheep and cows pass by through the car window, I reflected on how bizarre this was. Could this newfound freedom truly be mine? I could hardly believe it was real. Yet, I knew that one day, it would be Sinead's turn to leave, and when that day came, I was confident she would seek me out.

"Here, do ye smoke?" Mr Quinn asked, passing me a packet of cigarettes and a box of matches. His eyes focused on the road as he steered the car with one hand.

"I do. Thanks," I answered nervously.

"Light me one up as well," he said, smiling broadly. I returned the smile, took two cigarettes, lit them together, and passed the other one to him.

We had met for the first time when he'd picked me up at the convent. Sharing a smoke certainly helped to break the ice. The car was quickly filling with smoke. Mr Quinn wound the window down, and fresh air rushed in, whistling through the car and clearing the smoke in seconds. It felt good, brushing close to my face and blowing my hair about.

"Is that too cold for you, Frances?" he asked, winding the window up a little.

"No, it's fine." It was the first time he'd said my name, which sounded nice. I hadn't liked it when the nuns used it: they had a way of voicing 'Frances', which made it sound like a devastating insult. Although, they mostly referred to the girls by their number or surname.

I was beginning to relax with Mr Quinn. He appeared to be a decent man. His middle-aged, rugged appearance made me assume he lived in the countryside. He had short dark-brown hair and brown eyes. His suit had seen better days; he seemed like a typical Irishman. He was not unattractive but not as particular about his appearance as some men like to be. I hoped his family would be as easy to be around.

I casually chatted with him for the rest of our journey to Portadown. It was pleasant. We got to learn a bit about each other. Mr Quinn talked about his wife, who was still in hospital after giving birth to another son, their seventh child. He told me that he had only one daughter. There wasn't much of an age gap between the children, which was not unusual for a good Catholic family in Ireland. "With all the wee boys I have now, sure, I could start my own football team," he joked.

I learned that Mr Quinn owned a betting shop in the town. He seemed immensely proud of both his family and the betting shop.

"Sure, ye can help me count up my takings when I bring them home at the end of the day," he suggested.

When Mr Quinn asked me about my interests and hobbies, I confessed that what I loved more than anything was singing and Irish dancing. It was a passion my sisters and I shared and something we excelled at. Growing up under the care of nuns, with little else to occupy us, these pursuits were all we had, and we had dedicated ourselves to mastering them.

Despite the turmoil bubbling within me and the haunting memories of my time in the convent, I maintained a facade of composure in the presence of Mr Quinn. His admiration for the nuns and priests and their perceived dedication to the girls under their care was palpable. As he spoke glowingly of their commitment and praised their supposed good works, I nodded along dutifully, concealing the bitter truth that lay beneath the surface.

Mr Quinn's idealised image of the nuns mirrored the facade they presented to visitors, a carefully crafted illusion that obscured the darker realities we endured behind closed doors. Though tempted to shatter his naivety and expose the truth, I knew now was not the time or place. So, I continued to nod and feign agreement, masking my inner turmoil with a practised smile, all the while silently yearning for the day when I could break free from the chains of silence and speak the truth.

When Mr Quinn told me that my room, at the top of the house, was ready for me to move into, my heart leapt with anticipation. The lack of privacy in the convent had been suffocating, and the idea of having a space to call my own was like a dream come true. I looked forward to exploring my new sanctuary and revelling in its promised solitude.

The thought of no longer being subjected to the piercing sound of the morning bell was a relief. That bell had been rung every morning by a nun pacing up and down the dormitory. She would ring that bell with all her might until the last girl was out of bed and on their knees for prayers. The relentless routine of the convent, with its strict schedules and constant reminders of authority, was behind me now.

As the car rolled along the road, carrying me farther away from the convent with each passing mile, a glimmer of hope began to stir within me. The reality of leaving behind the only life I had ever known, with its harsh rules and relentless routine, filled me with a mixture of excitement and trepidation. For so long, I had resigned myself to existence within the convent walls. The prospect of stepping into the unknown and forging a new path for myself beyond those walls was daunting and exhilarating.

The mere possibility of freedom, of a life beyond the suffocating confines of convent life, was tantalising. Yet, even as hope blossomed within me, I remained guarded. Years of disappointment and disillusionment had instilled in me a sense of caution and a readiness to face life's inevitable challenges with resilience. I had learnt not to place my trust in others, relying solely on myself and my sister, Sinead. Despite my reservations, however, I couldn't suppress the flicker of hope urging me forward.

Although it was exciting to be out, I was also terrified. I had no idea what would be expected of me, and I was worried the Quinn family might not take to me. I'd been in care since I was two years old when my mother had abandoned my two sisters and me outside the gates of the Nazareth House Convent in Belfast. Being with a family would feel strange, and I'd had no time to adjust to this big change in my life. Not knowing if I would fit in made me extremely nervous. The uncertainty of what lay ahead weighed heavily on my mind as we neared the house.

After several hours of driving, we veered off the main road and approached a big old house. It stood amidst a vast patch of land encircled by a recently whitewashed wall. I thought someone needed to do a better job of it, as the paint was patchy with splashes of whitewash all over the ground.

There wasn't a typical driveway, just a rough gravel path created by years of cars driving over the land.

"Here we are now, Frances," Mr Quinn announced with relief as we approached an imposing three-story house.

I gazed out at the large green doors and counted eight large windows. I could see his children looking out of one of them, on the bottom floor, waving. They appeared happy with broad smiling faces.

Stepping out of the car, I couldn't help but notice the neglected feel of the place. The grounds surrounding the house lacked any semblance of care or attention. There were no flowers or lawns, just a vast expanse of untamed wilderness. It might have been left deliberately as a copious, wild space for the children to play in, but it needed something for them to play on.

Mr Quinn retrieved my small brown suitcase from the boot and handed it to me. It contained all my worldly possessions: a toothbrush, a hairbrush, a change of underwear, and a handful of second-hand clothes. Items graciously donated to me during my time at the convent. It wasn't much to embark on my new life with, but it was all I had.

Mr Quinn led me through the imposing green door and into the porch. In front of us was a set of glass-panelled doors. On the other side of them, I could see the children and a lady. Mr Quinn opened the door, and they all stared at me as we walked through. I felt extremely nervous.

"Hello, ye, must be Frances Reilly," the woman said, smiling as she reached out to shake my hand.

"Hello, yeah, I am Frances," I replied, shaking hands with her.

I imagined she was looking me up and down to see if I was suitable. I desperately wanted her approval as it would make it a lot easier for me to settle in.

"This is the children's Aunty Molly," Mr Quinn explained. "She's staying with us to help out while their mother is in hospital."

"I'll be showing ye to your room now, Frances, and then we can have some tea, and ye can tell us all about yourself."

Mr Quinn walked off with the children, leaving me to follow Molly across the enormous entrance hall's black and white mosaic-tiled floor. Twin staircases rose from either side of the entrance hall, meeting at the top of a landing. The stairs had the same black and white tiled flooring and black stained wooden bannisters. We reached the top and walked along the landing until we reached another stairway. I followed Molly up the narrow stairwell to the top floor.

"This will be your room!" Molly announced proudly as we approached an open door.

Stepping inside, I took in the sight of the room adorned with yellow floral wallpaper: its colours faded with time. The worn curtains, framing a small sash window, featured a larger yellow flower print. The furniture, much like the décor, bore the marks of age. A solitary wooden bed, neatly made with pillows, sheets, blankets, and a threadbare green counterpane, occupied one corner.

Against the opposite wall stood a small wooden wardrobe and a chest of drawers, their surfaces weathered from years of use. Though the room lacked vibrancy, it offered a sense of solace and privacy. The room might be drab, but it was my own space, and as I put my case beside the bed, I thought I'd make it more homely in time.

The kitchen was large and old-fashioned, with a welcoming fire roaring in the range. A large iron kettle whistled on top, and Molly quickly grabbed a tea towel and lifted it to fill the teapot.

I sat down at the big wooden table just as Mr Quinn appeared with the children. They were impatient to know when their mother would be out of the hospital with their new baby brother. "I'll be off to the hospital after my tea; maybe I'll find out then. Now, come and meet Frances. She's going to be looking after ye from now on."

He put his arm around the only girl among the children. "This is Margaret. She's named after her mother, and she's ten years old," Mr Quinn said proudly. Then he patted each of his sons on the head as he told me their names and ages: Peter, age eight: Thomas, age seven: Liam, age five: Michel, age four: and finally, Sean, age two.

"Hello, Frances," they all said in turn.

I smiled back at each one and said, "Hello, I am pleased to meet ye." They seemed to be friendly, well-mannered children.

Molly put plates of ham and egg sandwiches, which she'd prepared earlier, on the table and the family tucked in as she poured the tea.

Over tea, Molly and Mr Quinn quizzed me about the convent and myself. I answered as best as I could while refraining from speaking badly about the nuns, even if what I wanted to say was true.

Mr Quinn announced that I would accompany them to Mass every Sunday morning. The thought of stepping into a church again filled me with apprehension. After a lifetime spent in the regimented routine of chapel visits three times a day, along with morning and night prayers and prayers before and after meals, I had grown weary of the religious obligations imposed upon me. The harrowing experiences endured by my sisters and me under the care of the nuns had cast doubt on my faith in Catholicism.

Despite my reservations, I chose to keep my thoughts to myself. In the politically charged climate of Northern Ireland at that time, voicing one's doubts about religion was considered perilous. The region was sharply divided along sectarian lines, and individuals were expected to align themselves firmly as either Catholic or Protestant, with no room for ambiguity. It was a divisive issue that often dominated conversations, serving as a test for one's loyalties.

Under the strict teachings of Sister Thomas, we had been indoctrinated to believe that Catholicism was the sole path to salvation. Protestants were condemned to eternal damnation.

Suddenly, I was aware that everyone had gone quiet, and the family were staring at me. I imagined they must be waiting for some sign of my gratitude for not letting me miss Sunday Mass. I decided to go along with it, for now, and be thankful that it wouldn't be a daily routine.

"Frances, you'll be paid three pounds and ten shillings a week," Molly announced. "But ye will need to put some of it into a post office savings account for your clothes and other things ye will need. I'll show ye where the post office is."

I was pleased to get the money but needed to figure out what three pounds and ten shillings would buy. I'd never had any money to spend and had yet to learn of its value. It was strange to realise I would soon be able to buy items for myself: some decent clothes and bits and pieces for my room!

After tea, Mr Quinn stood up and announced he had to get to the hospital. Immediately, all the children began pestering him. "Can we go too? We want to see our wee baby brother!" Margaret insisted, but their father was firm. Their mammy needed some rest to get well enough to come home, and all of them turning up would only make her tired.

"Come on now, let your daddy be on his way, and we'll go for a long walk. I'm sure Frances would like to see a bit of the town," Molly suggested. The children didn't look impressed but obediently rushed to get their coats.

Molly walked us all around town for miles. She appeared to be in her element as she pointed out the children's schools, the Catholic church, Mr Quinn's betting-shop, the greengrocers and the butcher's shop that the family used.

By the time we arrived back at the house, the children were weary from the day's activities, and their stomachs rumbled with hunger. The fading daylight signalled the end of the day. Molly, ever the resourceful host, announced that she had prepared a shepherd's pie earlier, requiring only a quick reheat in the oven. We eagerly gathered around the kitchen table, engaged in lively conversation as we waited for the meal to be ready.

The kitchen exuded warmth, both from the comforting glow of the range and the congenial atmosphere shared among us. As we chatted, I took the opportunity to deepen my connection with the children, getting to know them better with each passing moment. Time seemed to slip away unnoticed until Molly served plates of piping hot shepherd's pie.

We wasted no time digging in, savouring each flavourful bite of the delicious meal. Molly's culinary prowess was evident in every mouthful, and I couldn't help but aspire to emulate her culinary skills someday.

Afterwards, it was fun listening to the children play 'I Spy' to pass the time until their daddy returned. Later, Molly told the children to get washed, brush their teeth and get into their pyjamas.

Just after nine o'clock, Mr Quinn returned home with news that his wife was expected to be discharged from the hospital in the morning, accompanied by their newborn baby. While uncertain about the exact time of their arrival, he reassured us that it would be after the doctor had completed his rounds. Molly's face lit up with joy upon hearing the news, expressing her excitement at the prospect of their reunion.

Mr Quinn nodded in agreement, acknowledging that Molly had already put the children to bed, not wishing to prolong their wait any further. He assured her he would share the good news with them in the morning, ensuring they were among the first to celebrate the happy occasion.

"I stopped off at the bookies and picked up the takings," Mr Quinn announced, dumping two cloth bags full of money on the table. "Frances, you can help me count them once I've looked in on the children."

Upon his return, Mr Quinn emptied the contents of the bags onto the kitchen table, a mixture of notes and coins cascading over its surface. It was staggering to witness the amount of money accumulated in just one day's work.

With practised ease, he demonstrated his preferred method of counting, arranging the notes in neat piles and instructing me to follow suit. Seated beside him, I watched carefully precisely how he did it. Years of experience had honed his skills to a high-speed precision, a stark contrast to my own cautious and somewhat hesitant approach. Fearful of making a mistake, I proceeded with caution, taking my time to ensure accuracy.

To my relief, Mr Quinn remained patient and understanding, offering words of encouragement. For him, the paramount concern was that the final tally added up correctly, regardless of the pace at which it was achieved. He reassured me saying that with practice I would soon speed up.

As Mr Quinn stepped away, leaving me alone in the kitchen with the money, a strange sensation washed over me. I had never been in the presence of such a substantial sum before, and the temptation to help myself to a few notes tugged at my conscience. My mouth felt dry and nerves fluttered in the pit of my stomach. Adrenaline surged through my veins, causing sweat to bead on my forehead.

At that moment, Sister Thomas's stern voice echoed in my mind, warning me of the consequences of succumbing to temptation. "You'll burn in hell, Reilly! God is always watching you," her words seemed to reverberate through my being, sending a shiver down my spine. I found myself frozen in place, unable to move.

Despite the temptation, I forced myself to focus on the task at hand and resumed counting. However, I couldn't help thinking how unfair it was that some people should have so much while others struggled to survive.

I was relieved when Mr Quinn returned, dispelling the temptation that had gripped me in his absence. With his reassuring presence by my side, we resumed the task and my earlier moment of weakness fading into the background.

As we neared the end of our tally, a thought crossed my mind: perhaps Mr Quinn had been testing my integrity all along, knowing full well the exact amount of money contained within the bag. It was a sobering realisation, one that underscored the importance of trust and honesty in our interactions.

Once the counting was complete, Molly kindly prepared some cocoa for us to enjoy. Mr Quinn graciously offered me the opportunity to retire to my room. Expressing my gratitude, I bid them both good night and ascended the stairs, leaving the kitchen behind as I made my way to my temporary sanctuary.

I sat on my bed, sipping my warm cocoa and allowing the day's happenings to drift through my mind. I found it challenging to process all the changes. I'd woken that morning to the sound of the nun's bell, and now I was in this grand house, with my own room, surrounded by a family I didn't know.

Thoughts of Sinead weighed heavily on my mind as I settled into my new surroundings. The guilt of embarking on this new chapter of my life while my younger sister remained trapped in that dreadful place gnawed at my conscience. Despite knowing deep down that I wasn't to blame for the circumstances that had unfolded, the burden of responsibility weighed heavily upon me.

Growing up in the convent, I had been conditioned to believe that experiencing any form of happiness or pleasure was inherently selfish, a sin that warranted confession on Fridays. Consequently, the conflicting emotions of joy and guilt which I now felt were making it difficult to embrace the positive changes in my life fully. Determined to alleviate some of that, I resolved to speak with Mr Quinn in the morning about visiting my sister.

I had been in bed for just a few minutes when I felt someone's hand on my shoulder.

"Come on, Frances. It's time to get up."

"But the bell hasn't gone yet," I mumbled. I sat up in bed and rubbed the sleep from my eyes. The light from the hall shone through the door, and I could see the silhouette of a woman standing beside the bed. For a moment, I sat disorientated and frightened. My eyes quickly scanned the room, and I remembered where I was.

"Come on now, it's six-thirty," Molly said, then she left the room.

I quickly washed and dressed, then headed downstairs. The house was quiet, and I found Molly in the kitchen, measuring porridge oats into a saucepan. "There's some tea and toast on the table; ye can help yourself," she said. I was relieved to see the toasted soda bread. The porridge in the convent had been awful: it was so hard you could cut it with a knife. I never wanted to eat porridge again.

Molly's voice echoed through the house as she called out the children's names from the foot of the stairs. "Come on now, your breakfast is ready!" she called one last time before retreating to the kitchen to tend to the breakfast.

As she stirred the steaming porridge on the stove, Molly turned her attention to me, outlining part of my new responsibilities. Taking the children to school would be part of my duties, she explained, and she offered to accompany me on the first morning to help me become familiar with the route.

Before long, the children began to trickle into the kitchen, their sleepy faces illuminated by the soft morning light. Margaret carried Sean with his legs clenched tightly around her waist, still looking half-asleep. The kitchen soon filled with the chatter and laughter of the Quinn children.

"Good morning," they said politely, then sat down.

"Good morning," I replied, getting up and holding my arms out to Sean. I had hoped he would respond and come to me so that Margaret could get her breakfast, but he looked away and wouldn't let go of his sister's neck."

"He'll come around in time," Molly said as she lifted Sean from Margaret's arms and settled him into his highchair. The Quinn household buzzed with anticipation as Molly shared the news of their mother and the baby's impending return. Excited chatter erupted from the children, their voices filled with joy and excitement.

With beaming faces hopeful anticipation, they pleaded with Molly for a day off school to welcome their mother and new sibling home. I silently hoped she would say yes, especially on this blustery, cold morning, which made the prospect of accompanying them to school less appealing. However, my hopes were dashed as Molly firmly denied their request, insisting that it was essential to maintain their routine.

You're going to school, and you can see your mammy and baby brother when you come home!" Mr Quinn's stern voice filled the room as he entered, his presence commanding attention. "Come on now, eat up your breakfast."

With a firm but gentle tone, he guided the children through their morning routine, ensuring they finished their meals before preparing for school. With a final word of encouragement, the children obediently dispersed, eager to begin their day.

Molly turned to me with a warm smile, requesting that I check on the children to see if they needed any assistance getting ready for school. It was a small task but one that underscored my growing role within the Quinn household.

Mr Quinn sat at the kitchen table, engrossed in the morning newspaper, as his children bid him farewell with kisses before heading off to school. With a sense of curiosity tinged with concern, I couldn't help but wonder why he hadn't offered them a lift in his car, especially on such a bitterly cold morning.

Bundled up against the biting chill, Molly and I joined the children on their trek to school, undeterred by the frosty weather. Despite the cold, the children excitedly debated what to name the baby, each offering their own suggestions. Their lively chatter served as a delightful diversion from the wintry conditions.

Our first stop was Margaret's convent school, followed by dropping off Peter and Thomas at the boys' Catholic school. Finally, we delivered Liam and Michel to the nursery, ensuring each child reached their destination safely before hastily retreating from the biting cold.

"I'll not be needed now Mrs Quinn is coming home," Molly informed me, "And I'll be glad to get home to see my husband and friends."

She seemed pleased, but I felt selfishly disappointed. I was afraid I wasn't ready for the job before me: I needed more time to settle in and learn my responsibility. Also, I got on well with Molly and wanted her to stay and guide me. However, it was hard not to feel at least a little pleased for her, as she clearly missed her family and friends. Somehow, I was just going to have to manage without her.

On our return, we found Mr Quinn and Sean playing on the floor with a toy garage, a lorry and some cars. There were a lot of traffic sounds being made by them both, as they pushed the vehicles along. We warmed ourselves by the range with a cup of tea while we watched them play. I hadn't realised how much I'd missed out on not having a family. There had been no one to play with me growing up. I felt envious of the children in this house. They had no idea how fortunate they were.

Molly asked what I was daydreaming about, then said we should finish our tea before I had a chance to answer. "We have to get the housework done before Mrs Quinn arrives home from the hospital," she explained. She took me to a large cupboard full of cleaning supplies and explained that I should start at the top of the house and work my way down.

Carrying a bucket brimming with cleaning supplies, along with a mop and floor brush, I ascended to the top floor of the house, ready to tackle the daunting task of cleaning each room with meticulous care. I worked my way through the bedrooms before moving on to the bathroom, landings, and stairs. Working without the nuns watching over me was great, but I still worked just as hard as I had in the convent.

As I scrubbed and polished each surface, my thoughts lingered on the importance of impressing Mrs Quinn with the quality of my work. The prospect of returning to the convent loomed in the back of my mind. I hoped that my efforts would be enough to secure my place in the Quinn household for good.

Later, I heard Mr Quinn leave the house and heard the car driving away.

I had almost finished the lower stairs when Molly shouted, "Frances, ye can take a wee break now. There's a cup of tea and a sandwich here for ye on the kitchen table."

I carried the mop and bucket with me down to the kitchen. "Thanks, Molly!" I was very grateful for the break.

Molly left the kitchen to put Sean down for a nap and returned with a surprised expression on her face. "Well, ye certainly know how to clean Frances. You've done a grand job upstairs!"

I wasn't used to praise and was unsure how to respond. I said nothing, but I could feel the heat from my face blushing.

"There's just the downstairs rooms left to do now when ye had your tea. Mrs Quinn won't be home for a few hours yet."

There were a few minutes left to enjoy sitting in the kitchen's warmth, and I wanted to make the most of it. The rest of the house was much colder, although the hard work had helped to warm me up. As we finished our tea, Molly inquired, with more questions about my life in the convent. She told me Mr Quinn was her brother, and their sister, Teresa, was a nun in the south of Ireland. Once again, I felt uncomfortable with the conversation, knowing I couldn't be honest about my feelings.

By the time I had completed all the cleaning and various other jobs, it was time to go and collect the children from school. Molly got Sean ready to accompany us. "The fresh air will do him good," she insisted. "Maybe your mammy and daddy will be here when we get back," she told Sean, using that silly sing-song voice people often use when talking to babies.

Fortunately, the air was much warmer now than on the morning walk, and being out of the house for a while was pleasant. The children were eager to get home and rushed ahead of us. They weren't disappointed when Molly told them their mother had not yet returned home with the baby, as they felt sure their parents would be back by the time they got home. Margaret, determined to be the first to see the baby, skipped along the road ahead of the rest, with the boys struggling to keep up. Then suddenly, they all started to run to see who could get to the house first. Molly carried Sean as we rushed along behind.

"They're home!" the children shouted as soon as they could see the car and dashed to the front door, making a commotion. "Calm down, you lot, or you'll frighten the baby," Molly shouted after them.

I felt very apprehensive about meeting Mrs Quinn, perhaps because she would be my boss. I stopped momentarily, took a deep breath and braced myself before going inside. I'd already formed a good feeling about the rest of the family, and the excitement of the children and her husband at her return had reassured me somewhat. She must be a nice person, I reasoned. But, after the convent, it would take time for me to truly trust anything about this family.

"Ye look terrified, Frances. Come on in, ye'll, be fine," Molly insisted, reading my mind.

Mrs Quinn was in bed, and everyone had gathered in her room. It was the only bedroom on the ground floor. The door was open, and I could see Mr Quinn, Molly and the children around the bed, but they blocked my view of Mrs Quinn. The baby was crying as they all stood around looking at him. I went to the kitchen to warm myself but also because I didn't want to be found gawking in at them. I was glad of the warmth of the range and a bit of time on my own to gather my thoughts. It was well over half an hour before anyone came into the kitchen. Molly's voice and a loud thudding noise disturbed my thoughts. "Will ye peel these spuds for dinner, Frances?" she asked, tipping the potatoes from her apron into the sink.

"Yeah, surely. Do ye want me to do all of them?"

"Yeah, and be sure you cut them all the same size, or some will be done before the rest are ready."

I found myself a sharp knife and the largest saucepan and got to work on them immediately. As I peeled the potatoes, Molly asked if I'd cooked at the convent, and I told her I hadn't.

"Well, I hope ye learn quickly because you'll have to cook while you're here," she warned me.

I suddenly felt very sick as I hadn't known that I would be expected to cook. Cooking was probably the only thing we didn't have to do in the convent. If we had, the food would have been much better.

"I'll show ye how to make tonight's dinner; it's sausage, mash and peas. If ye listen and watch carefully, then ye'll know the next time." I thanked her and obediently did as she asked: watching and listening carefully as she explained everything to me.

When dinner was served, Mr Quinn asked if I would make up a tray for his wife and take it to her. Terrified, I paused outside her bedroom door and tried to stop the tray from shaking. I was so nervous that I was sure I would drop the tray and our first meeting would be a disaster. Taking a deep breath, I gripped the tray firmly with one hand and then knocked on the door. "Come in," invited a friendly voice.

In contrast to other parts of the house, the room was comfortably furnished and a raging open coal fire ensured that the room was pleasantly warm. Mrs Quinn lay on a large, old-fashioned, wooden bed propped up with half a dozen soft pillows. She was an attractive woman of fair complexion splashed with freckles. She had long, thick jet-black curly hair and was slightly chubby. "You must be Frances. I hope you're settling in, okay," she asked.

"Yes, I am. Thank you," I said, with a smile.

Placing the tray down in front of her, I caught sight of the baby sleeping in a cot beside her bed. He looked peaceful and incredibly fragile. "His name's Leo," she announced with a tone of majesty.

"He's absolutely gorgeous," I whispered nervously while exiting the room. I had expected Mrs Quinn to be arrogant and intimidating, like a Reverend Mother but she seemed nice although a little snobby. I had a good feeling about working for her.

After dinner, as Mr Quinn went to collect the day's earnings and the children conversed with their mother, I resumed my chores in the kitchen.

Molly made us both another cup of tea and told me she'd be leaving, in about an hour, when her husband arrived. While we drank our tea, she explained that once the children were ready for bed their socks and pants had to be washed out, ready for the morning. I was to wash them in the sink, on a washboard, then wring then out tightly and hang them a wooden rack which pulled down from the ceiling above the range. She rose from the table and showed me how to lower it using a rope. It was similar to the ones in the laundry at the convent, only much smaller.

Molly looked happy to be going home. She told me that she didn't have any children of her own and was pleased to be able to help her brother out. I thought she appeared tired and would be glad to get home for a rest. There was a lot to do at the Quinn house, and she had certainly done her bit.

When the doorbell rang Molly rushed to answer it. A few moments later, she returned with her husband. "This is Frances," she said.

"Hello, Frances, I'm Uncle Frank." He sounded warm and friendly as he reached across to take my hand. Molly poured him a cup of tea and put out some cake on a plate. He looked delighted to be collecting Molly and taking her home.

As they were leaving, I stood at the front door waving goodbye along with the children. As Molly and Frank drove away I felt overwhelmed at being left to cope on my own and wished I'd been able to spend more time with Molly: getting used to the children and learning what was expected of me, especially how to cook. But I knew that, somehow, I would have to cope or else I would be back in the convent.

Molly brewed another round of tea and informed me of the evening's laundry routine. As she prepared to leave upon her husband's return, she expressed her satisfaction in helping her brother's family despite her weariness.

As Molly departed with her husband, I stood on the doorstep, waving goodbye. The weight of responsibility settled heavily upon my shoulders. Without Molly's steady guidance, the job before me felt overwhelming. In particular, the thought of mastering simple tasks felt daunting, particularly tasks like cooking, which were still foreign to me.

Despite my trepidation, I knew I had no choice but to adapt. The thought of returning to the oppressive and regimented life of the convent was unbearable.

Missing Molly

Before Mr Quinn returned home with the day's takings, I busied myself with the evening routine, helping the children bathe and get ready for bed. Once they were settled, I turned my attention to preparing a tray of tea and biscuits for Mrs Quinn.

Then, with my tasks complete and the children settled down, quiet finally settling over the house. With nothing more left to do, I switched on the small black and white TV in the kitchen and caught up with some of the day's news. The fuzzy picture but this was one of the many pleasures I had been unable to enjoy in the convent. It was a small but significant reminder of the newfound sense of independence I was beginning to experience in this new chapter of my life.

Watching the news, I realised, for the first time, just how much the Catholics and Protestants communities hated each other. Even the government officials couldn't control their anger and resentment. I didn't understand much of what they'd been talking about, but it was clear that they all expected the situation to worsen.

At that moment, I couldn't help but feel a sense of profound sadness and disillusionment at the thought of such deep-seated hatred tearing communities apart. It was a sobering realisation that forced me to confront the harsh realities of the world outside the convent walls.

Just then, Mr Quinn came to the kitchen and asked if I would make him tea. "Those bloody Prods," he remarked, clearly angry. I was filling the kettle and turned around to see who he was talking to. His eyes were fixed on the television. I felt awkward and embarrassed for not understanding his comment and wasn't sure how to respond if a response was needed. I had no feelings toward Protestants one way or the other. I didn't know what they had done wrong that was so bad. However, it was clear I would have to stay away from them, or there could be trouble.

Mr Quinn put the bags of money on the kitchen table. "We'll count this all up after I've popped in to see how my wife's doing. Frances, you could polish the children's shoes while you're waiting. My wife will run you through your duties tomorrow," he explained, walking off with his cup of tea.

I found the shoe polish and brushes in the cleaning cupboard and started polishing. I felt mentally and physically exhausted and would have liked to go to my room and fall onto my bed. It had been a long day.

As I polished, my attention was drawn to the bags of money on the table and the temptation which I'd felt the previous evening returned. Again, I wondered whether Mr Quinn was testing me or trusting me.

Then I thought about God watching my every move; it seemed as though I could feel his eyes upon me with that the temptation soon passed. This was very strange and unexpected for me as I had developed very strong doubts about God, religion and all the teachings of the nuns. I guessed that years of brainwashing, in the convent, must still be affecting me even if I had stopped believing.

By the time we finally got around to counting the money it was already twenty past ten. Despite my efforts to remain alert and focused, the late hour and long day had taken their toll, and I was finding it increasingly difficult to remain focused and not yawn. By eleven o'clock I was desperately tired, and it was a tremendous relieved when we had finished tallying the money, and Mr Quinn told me that I could go to my room.

"Here ye are now Frances, you'll be needing this to get ye up in the morning," he said and handed me an alarm clock.

"Thank you, Mr Quinn."

"The children will be having porridge for breakfast. Good night, Frances, and God bless."

"Good night, Mr Quinn."

Exhausted, I sank onto my bed and set the alarm for six o'clock. Too tired to dwell on the events of the day, I began to undress. Thoughts of Sinead crossed my mind again, and I realised I hadn't had a chance to discuss visiting her with anyone. She probably thought I was having a grand time and had forgotten about her. While that wasn't the case, I could understand her feeling that way, as it was a common assumption whenever someone left. I made a mental note to ask Mr Quinn in the morning when I could visit her.

I jolted awake to the blaring sound of the alarm and hurried across the room to silence it. Standing there for a moment, I rubbed my eyes to shake off the drowsiness. The room was freezing, and the temptation to crawl back into the warmth of my bed was strong. "Just five more minutes," I thought, especially since there were no nuns around to reprimand me. But I fought off the urge: if I had succumbed, the children would have been late for school, and I would have faced consequences, perhaps even a return to the convent. For a fleeting moment, I allowed myself to imagine the luxury of waking up naturally and rising when I pleased. But reality quickly set in, and I pushed aside such fantasies, focusing instead on getting washed and dressed as quickly as possible.

In the kitchen, a glorious heat radiated from the range. Mr Quinn must have stoked it up thoroughly before going to bed. I filled the kettle and put it on top of the range. First, I would have some tea, and then I'd try to make the porridge. I remembered watching Molly when she'd made it and tried to remember how many cups she'd used. It can't be that hard, I told myself. Seven cups of porridge went into a saucepan, then hot water from the kettle and some milk.

I remembered Molly had used salt, so I shook and shook until I thought I'd put enough in, and then I stirred it all together with a wooden spoon. Feeling very proud of myself, I then placed it on the range. While sitting down for my tea and toast, I heard the porridge bubbling nicely. I still had plenty of time to call the children.

Once I'd washed my breakfast dishes, I went to the saucepan to stir the porridge. Luckily, I'd used the big saucepan because, by now, the amount of porridge had more than tripled and was so thick that I struggled to move the wooden spoon through it. I was having a panic attack, hoping no one would see my efforts until I could try to rescue it. I thought it needed more water and milk, so I poured the rest from the kettle and a half-pint of milk. It wasn't easy at first, but the spoon soon began to move through the porridge. I pounded the lumps so they would break up and blend in with the rest of the porridge.

Eventually, after more stirring, I thought it looked okay, even if there appeared to be enough to feed a classroom full of children. My porridge smelled more delicious than the sludge I'd had to endure daily in the convent, but I really should have tasted it. Unfortunately, just thinking about that reminded me of the convent food and made me want to gag. I was so satisfied that the porridge was saved that I went upstairs to wake the children. I felt incredibly proud of myself for making breakfast. It made me feel like an adult.

The children were very responsive and jumped straight out of bed. They knew the morning routine, and Margaret kindly offered to help me with the little ones until they got used to me.

"Good morning!" Mr Quinn's voice made me jump. As I served up the porridge, he smiled at me to show his approval. A look that suggested I was working out nicely.

"Yuck, it's horrible," Margaret screeched, spitting the porridge back into her bowl. Mr Quinn stared sternly at her.

"That's not very polite, Margaret."

As the other children took hesitant bites of the porridge, their expressions quickly turned sour, and one by one, they began to grimace and spit out their mouthfuls. I watched in dismay as Mr Quinn's face contorted in horror, his initial shock giving way to a mixture of disbelief and frustration.

Rushing to investigate the source of the commotion, Mr Quinn grabbed a spoon and sampled the porridge for himself. His reaction was immediate and emphatic.

"Oh, my good God, that's awful, Frances! What were you thinking? Who taught ye to make porridge like this, and how much of this have ye made?"

His words struck me like a physical blow, and I felt a wave of embarrassment wash over me as I struggled to find a response. Caught off guard by Mr Quinn's outburst, I blurted out an apology. It was clear that my attempt at recreating Molly's recipe had fallen far short of expectations.

"I'm sorry, I don't know how to cook. I've tried my best," I blurted out in frustration, barely holding back my tears.

Mr Quinn told me not to get upset and cleared away the bowls. "Make some toast for the children; ye can do that, can't ye!" he demanded.

I felt inadequate and stupid and worried again that I'd be sent back to the convent. I knew that if this didn't work out, I would be returned to the nuns as I was still officially under their care.

The atmosphere remained tense, and Mr Quinn spoke to me only to demand something. When the children were ready for me to walk them to school, he said goodbye to them and stormed off across the hallway to see his wife.

I heard him through the door saying, "Ye know, I thought those convent girls were used to working hard and could do whatever was required of them. It's no bloody good if she can't fucking cook!"

The children could also hear: it was loud enough. Maybe I was meant to hear that he was furious. I had now seen another side of Mr Quinn and realised that I couldn't trust anything about my current situation. Had the nuns not told them what I could and couldn't do because I'd never been taught to cook? I was distraught but tried, for the children's benefit, not to let it show. It was a quiet walk to school that morning.

As the days turned into months, I grew accustomed to the demanding routine of household chores. From washing sheets to uniforms and even Mr and Mrs Quinn's clothing; every task demanded meticulous attention to detail. Mrs Quinn's exacting standards left little room for error, and any deviation from her expectations meant starting over from scratch.

Armed with only a washboard and a large sink, I would scrub each item of clothing until my hands were raw and tinged with red. The physical toll of this laborious process was matched only by the mental strain of ensuring that every garment met Mrs Quinn's exacting standards.

After washing, I would wring out each item by hand, a monotonous ritual that left my muscles aching and my fingers trembling. Then, I would then shake out each piece of clothing, striving to banish every crease and wrinkle before hanging them on the makeshift clothesline.

The weight of the wet garments would strain the flimsy line, threatening to snap it at any moment. To prevent disaster, I would prop it up with a wooden pole, a makeshift solution to a problem that could easily have been solved with modern conveniences like a washing machine.

I couldn't help but feel a sense of indignation at the Quinns' reluctance to invest in labour-saving devices. It seemed incomprehensible to me that they would choose to burden me with such arduous tasks when a simple machine could accomplish the same work in a fraction of the time.

Despite how hard I worked; Mrs Quinn always managed to find more for me to do. I began to wonder if she spent her time in bed thinking about how she could wring more work out of me. There were days when I didn't even have time to stop and get something to eat. And, when I did stop for lunch, she always seemed to ring that damn bell she had kept by her bed. She would lie in bed all day, constantly ringing for me, and it was driving me mad.

Just before Mr Quinn would return home in the evening, Mrs Quinn would appear out of her room, fully dressed, as if she'd been up all day. I found her infuriating! I was feeling very alone and missed Molly. She could have advised me on what to do. I wondered why people would have so many children if they didn't want to care for them. It was always late by the time I got to bed.

I felt constantly exhausted as they squeezed the last bit of work out of me, and there was no time left for myself. Unfortunately, my life had improved only marginally since leaving the convent, and I was worried that I would never be anything more than somebody's skivvy. With each new day, I became increasingly depressed.

Sunday morning mass at the local Catholic church was our only opportunity to dress up smartly. Mr and Mrs Quinn would drive the younger children, while I left earlier with the older ones, meeting them at the church. When it rained, all the children crammed into the car, and Mr Quinn kindly offered me an umbrella. Strangely, I found solace in the rain as it afforded me rare moments alone. Mass became a spectacle, with affluent parishioners looking down their noses at the less fortunate. A far cry from Christian values. It felt like a display of 'I'm better than you,' underscored by constant whispering and gossiping.

Whenever Mr and Mrs Quinn introduced me to others, they'd casually mention my origins in the orphanage as if suggesting one could pick a child like me, like picking out a horse. I overheard remarks about how 'convent girls' would obediently comply with any instruction given. Shockingly, I once heard a man brag about hiring one, insinuating little payment was necessary. It left me feeling disheartened, walking away as their sneers lingered in the air behind me.

"As the priest referred to us as 'his flock', I found myself questioning why he likened people to sheep. I was reluctant to mindlessly follow others without understanding the rationale behind it. Though familiar with the term 'flock', its significance deepened in that moment. My upbringing in the convent had already instilled a sense of scepticism within me, and the behaviour of certain congregation members, coupled with the rhetoric of this priest, only increased my growing distance from religion."

It was another dreary Monday morning, and it was raining hard as I returned from dropping the kids off at school. Dripping wet, I shook my coat hard at the back door, then hung it over the back of a chair, facing the range, to dry. Gathering all my cleaning products in the bucket and grabbing the mop and brush, I rushed upstairs to get changed out of my wet clothes.

No sooner had I started cleaning on the top landing than Mrs Quinn summoned me once more! "Not that damned bell again," I thought, but I still rushed to see what she wanted. I paused outside her door to brace myself, then knocked and prepared a fake smile for my entrance.

"Come on in," she answered, in a tone that once again suggested she was a lady of the manor and I was the nuisance maid, even though she was the demanding nuisance. When I entered the room, she was lounging on the bed, reading a magazine. "I'll have my morning tea and biscuits now," she ordered without raising her head from the article she was reading.

I felt like telling her to get up from her fat lazy ass and make her own bloody tea, but instead, as politely as my mood would allow, I whispered, "Yes, Mrs Quinn."

When I returned with her tray, she gave me a fresh list of jobs: clean the brass door knocker, take the mats outside and shake them, and then bring her a fresh cup of tea. Anything, it seemed, to distract me from what I was already working on. She must have known it would mean a lot of extra work for me and that my day was already crammed. As I left her room full of anger and frustration, tears welled in my eyes, and I decided, at that moment, to get as far away from Mrs Quinn as I could. I never wanted to hear her or that damn bell again. I wasn't going to take this any longer, and I wasn't going to wait until she called the nuns. This situation was no longer bearable.

As I sat there, my mind shifted into flight mode, swiftly concocting a plan to extricate myself from this intolerable predicament. It dawned on me at that moment that it was payday. Over time, I had diligently stashed away most of my earnings in a post office account. Week after week, I would allocate a portion for essentials—cigarettes, biscuits, writing paper, and stamps for corresponding with Sinead. Each letter was meticulously crafted, knowing full well they would be scrutinised by the watchful eyes of the nuns. Amidst the chaos, I had neglected to find time to spend the surplus.

I was confident there would be sufficient funds to facilitate my escape. This decision triggered a familiar sensation, one I had grown accustomed to. Anticipation tinged with trepidation, reminiscent of the moments just before I would flee the confines of the convent. It was a potent mix of exhilaration, at the prospect of freedom, and apprehension, stemming from the lack of control over one's fate. Despite the uncertainty, there was an undeniable attraction to living moment by moment, fuelling my adrenaline.

Ideally, I would have preferred not to resort to running, longing instead for the ideal job. Yet, the knowledge that I was not solely responsible for the predicament I found myself in provided some semblance of justification for what I was contemplating. I felt confident that I would secure another job before the police caught up with me. I harboured dreams, and conceding defeat was simply not in my nature.

I had come to realise, some months ago, that I would never see Sinead for as long as I stayed with the Quinns. They had always fobbed me off when I'd ask about visiting my sister. Despite my excitement, the day dragged along slowly, but a plan had formed in my mind.

Before heading to pick up the children from school that afternoon, I meticulously packed my belongings, ensuring everything was in order before placing my suitcase at the foot of my bed. It had become routine for Mrs Quinn to settle my wages before my departure to collect the children on Fridays. This allowed me to promptly deposit the funds into my post office account on my way to the school. However, today would be different. I intended to withdraw the money instead of making a deposit.

As I went about my tasks, preparing the tea tray with a hint of satisfaction. Knowing it would be the last time I performed this duty for Mrs Quinn, a sense of anticipation tinged with liberation filled the air. With the tray in hand, I made my way to her room, mustering a polite smile as I entered. Mrs Quinn handed me the familiar small brown envelope containing my wages. I expressed my gratitude before casting a final glance back at her, pondering who would now undertake the thankless work I had left behind.

Slowly and quietly, I crept downstairs and out the front door with my case tightly held. Once outside, I hid the suitcase behind a tree on the edge of the house's grounds. Next, I stopped at the post office and withdrew all my savings. Five months' savings was a lot of money to me. Then, I collected the children from their schools.

On the way back, trying hard to concentrate on what the children were talking about took a lot of effort as my mind was focused on getting away. I was frightened but didn't want to let that change my mind. Somehow, I managed to make the right noises for the children to believe that I was listening thoroughly to their stories.

As we approached the house, my heart was racing. "Will ye all go into the house, and I'll be in soon?" I asked. "I've something to do first." I wouldn't say I liked deceiving the children, it was not their fault, but I needed my plan to work. They did as I asked, and as I watched the door shut behind them, I whispered, "Goodbye." I imagined that, in some spiritual way, they would know I'd said it before I left. I hoped that they might understand, if they ever gave a thought as to why I had left.

"This is it, time to go," I told myself, grabbing my case. I ran away from the house as quickly as possible and didn't stop until I got a stitch in my side and could run no further. It wasn't too far to the bus depot now, maybe half a mile, and I carried on walking as fast as I could. "Is there a bus to Omagh?" I asked a conductor as he stepped off his bus.

"Yeah, that coach over there goes all the way without stops, but it doesn't leave for fifteen minutes," he said, pointing in its direction. I walked across to it and noticed the doors were open, but it was empty. I knew Mrs Quinn would have realised I was missing by now, and I was concerned that she, or her friends, would be out looking for me. So, I got on the coach and hid, slumped down in the back seat.

Nervous, butterfly feelings began to grow in the pit of my stomach. I realised I'd never travelled on a coach by myself before. I had been on one a few times before when I was young, and the Murphy family had taken me on holiday to their farm. Now, I was still trying to get used to the everyday things that most people took for granted. Things like going to the shops, getting on transport, talking to people and using money. I was still struggling to figure out what things cost. It was all alien to me and sometimes scary.

As I sat, cigarette in hand, waiting for the bus to depart, I tried to ease my nerves and relax in the warm, comforting confines of the coach. Despite the anonymity of my surroundings, Omagh held a special allure for me: it was my birthplace, a town where I felt an undeniable sense of belonging.

During my time in the convent, the nuns had discovered that I still had family residing in Omagh. While they were aware of my sisters and me, they had never made any effort to locate or reach out to us. It wasn't until discussions ensued between the nuns and myself that my younger sister and I were granted permission to stay with our Aunty Mary in Omagh. However, I later discovered that Aunty Mary had only agreed to take us in because the nuns had compensated her. Their intention was for her to care for us during their retreat period. While most of the other girls were reunited with their families during this time, my sister and I were normally left behind, feeling unwanted and unloved.

Aunty Mary, my mother's elder sister, rarely spoke of my mother, and when she did, it was never in a favourable light. She, along with the rest of the family, had severed ties with my mother before I reached the age of two. My mother's actions had caused considerable strife, bringing embarrassment and anger to the family. At times, her behaviour crossed into cruelty, leaving wounds that ran deep. Though I could never understand my mother's motivations, it was clear that her actions had driven a permanent wedge between her and her family.

Whenever Aunty Mary delved into my mother's past, it was with disdain, devoid of any shred of empathy. She cautioned me against seeking out my mother, painting her as irredeemable. She recounted my mother's tumultuous relationships with countless men, even suggesting that my siblings and I all have different fathers. The revelations cut deep. While part of me wondered if my mother deserved such scorn, I questioned the necessity of knowing such painful truths. Perhaps my mother had changed over time, softened by the passage of years.

Despite my hopes for reconciliation, Aunty Mary seemed fixated on the fear that my sister and I would follow in our mother's footsteps, haunted by the spectre of her past transgressions.

The rejection from my other aunts and uncles in Omagh, all due to my mother's actions, left me resentful of being judged by her mistakes. The thought of seeking their assistance now was disheartening, but I felt trapped with few alternatives. Besides my sister, Sinead, they were the only family I had left. Yet, even if they turned me away, the prospect of returning to Mr and Mrs Quinn's home was utterly unthinkable.

As the driver finally boarded the coach and passengers began to file in, a wave of relief washed over me. I had managed to slip onto the bus unnoticed. The conductor made his rounds, collecting fares. I breathed a sigh of relief, lit a cigarette and relaxed for the long journey ahead.

As the coach pulled away from the station, the tension slowly melted away with each passing mile. With nothing but the open road stretching out before me, I allowed myself to relax, sinking into the seat as the landscape blurred past the window. Soon, I started to wonder what life had in store for me next. I had to admit, I felt I was already becoming addicted to the buzz of being on the run.

Though it was likely that word of my disappearance had already spread, I refused to dwell on the consequences of my actions. After all, I had survived being on the run several times before.

Freedom

By the time the coach pulled into the bus station at Omagh, I was desperate to get out of that smoke-filled environment. Stepping out into the crisp, fresh air and stretching my legs after the lengthy journey felt wonderful. The town bustled with activity as people went about their shopping and daily routines. I wandered around for a while before entering The Golden Griddle Cafe for a cup of tea and a slice of apple pie with fresh cream. It was a delicious treat, but I knew that I should be flying under the radar for now as I assumed the police in Omagh, as well as in Portadown, could be on the lookout for me by now.

As I sat in the cafe, idly watching the ebb and flow of pedestrians passing by, a sense of apprehension gnawed at the edges of my mind. The prospect of facing Aunty Mary filled me with a mixture of dread and uncertainty, knowing all too well that her reception would likely be less than welcoming.

Finishing off the last crumbs of my apple pie, I couldn't help but wonder about my Aunty Mary's potential reaction to my unexpected arrival. I wondered what on earth I would say. I knew she wouldn't be pleased to see me on her doorstep. The thought of being turned away weighed heavily on my mind. The notion that she would take me in felt hopelessly optimistic, but I had to try.

With a deep breath, I steeled myself for the confrontation ahead, knowing that delaying the inevitable would only prolong the agony. Gathering my resolve, I rose from my seat, made my way out of the cafe and made my way up the Derry Road to her house.

The closer I got, the worse I felt, almost bottling out several times. I tried to convince myself everything would be fine, knowing this was only wishful thinking. However, I wasn't in the convent anymore and maybe my aunt, knowing what a hard worker I was, would give me a chance. The nuns would be happy with this arrangement, I thought, if I found some work. Eventually, I found myself standing outside my aunt's house. Feeling sick, I lit a cigarette to calm my nerves. I'd been pacing back and forth in her back garden, gathering the courage to knock on her door, when I heard a car pull up on the road beside the house. I peered around to see if my aunt was there.

"Is that you, Frances? Jesus, Mary and St. Joseph, what are you doing hanging around here?" I recognised the voice immediately. It was Uncle Jerry, looking very puzzled at seeing me.

"Could I see my Aunty Mary, please, Jerry?" was all I could say.

Jerry parked the car. As we walked to the door, I noticed him looking around to see if the neighbours had spotted me. They didn't like people knowing that Sinead and I were family. My Aunt Mary had told everyone we were poor orphans to whom they'd given a few holidays. They thought that made them seem like good Christians, but it made us feel even more miserable and unwanted.

Jerry opened the front door and called out to his wife. I followed him to the living room, where Mary sat by the fire. The sight of me brought her swiftly to her feet. "Look who I found hanging around outside," accused Jerry. "She was asking to see ye, Mary.

Mary invited me to sit down and then made some tea. Meanwhile, Jerry sat in his favourite chair and filled his pipe, trying to avoid eye contact with me. When Mary returned with three mugs, he acted like I wasn't there. "Is this a quick visit, Frances?" she asked sharply.

"No, I had to leave my job: the people I worked for weren't treating me well," I replied and tried to explain my situation to her.

"Ye can't afford to be fussy when ye need a roof over your head," she lectured me. "Sure, you've got nowhere else to go. Ye can thank your mother for that; now, beggars can't be choosers. Ye should know that by now, Frances."

"Yeah, I know, but I was no better off there than I was at the convent," I told my aunt. Tears began to form in my eyes, but I held them back. Mary said nothing, and she sat sternly, watching me as I sipped the tea. Instead, Jerry and my aunt exchanged disapproving looks. I took this to mean that I wouldn't be welcome here. It was what I expected. I shouldn't have come.

"Would you like me to go to the phone box and call the nuns?" Mary suggested, her voice tinged with condescension. "They would come and fetch you, Frances. Perhaps it would be best to go back with them. At least then, you'd have a roof over your head while they found you another job. And you'd be reunited with Sinead!"

"No, thank you. I can call them myself if I decide to. I just want to give this place a chance first. Please don't worry about me, Mary. I'll find a live-in job somewhere," I replied.

"The nuns might be better at finding you work with the right kind of people, but just like your mother, you won't listen to good advice," Mary persisted, her frustration evident.

"You always bring up my mother, and I don't even know who she is," I retorted. "And when you say, 'the right kind of people,' do you mean good Catholics like yourself? Hypocrites, the lot of you."

With that, I stormed out, slamming the front door behind me. Anger and sadness welled up inside me as I realised that my only relatives outside of the convent seemed indifferent to my and Sinead's well-being. Determined to prove them wrong, I vowed to find work in Omagh and make my own way without their help. Tears clouded my vision as I hurried back toward the town, feeling alone and abandoned.

Distracted and upset, I was thinking about what I should do next, so I didn't notice the two boys crossing the road behind me, shouting.

"Hang on, Frances, will ye wait a wee minute? Hang on, wait up."

Turning to see who was making all that racket while wiping my tears on my sleeve, I saw George and Kieran, who lived in the housing estate across from my aunty's house. They were part of a group of boys whom Sinead and I used to hang out with when we came here on holiday. George liked me a lot; I knew that because he'd told my sister several times that he would marry me one day. He said he didn't care how long he had to wait. She found that amusing and, bent over with laughter, insisted that it would never happen.

I hadn't taken him seriously, but it didn't stop him from telling everyone I was his girlfriend. I didn't correct him since I was a girl, and we were friends. I was naive and vulnerable and had never had anyone interested in me before. We would muck about or hang out by the telephone box, sitting on the brick wall chatting, until Sinead and I had to be in at nine-thirty in the evening. George was slim, had dark hair and blue eyes, and was attractive.

As they got closer, Kieran asked me what was wrong. I couldn't hide that I was upset and felt embarrassed. It certainly didn't help that they were seeing me like this. I was desperate now that I knew my aunt wouldn't help, so I told them everything. They walked along with me, and we tried to decide what I should do next.

In town, we encountered Paddy, a familiar face in our group. Paddy's vibrant ginger hair and speckled skin made him easily recognisable. Known for his playful nature, he was a natural joker who enjoyed light-hearted antics. However, there was one incident that left a lasting impression on me.

Once, in a moment of mischievousness, Paddy decided to chase me down the Derry Road with a large, wriggling worm in hand. The sight of it sent me into a panic, and I sprinted away in terror until I was physically incapable of running any further. By the time Paddy realised the extent of my distress, my face was pale with fear, and I was rendered speechless by shock. He swiftly dropped the worm, understanding the severity of my reaction.

It was during this incident that I first became aware of my severe phobia of worms. Despite my fear, I harbour no ill will towards Paddy. I couldn't help but chuckle whenever he playfully reminded me of the episode. However, there was one occasion where his teasing hit a nerve, prompting me to deliver a playful yet firm punch in response.

The four of us decided to head to the Rex cafe for some tea and conversation. Paddy kindly suggested that I stay at his house for a few nights until I could get things sorted out. "I'll need to check with me ma first," he mentioned, "but I reckon she'd be keen to lend a hand." I had visited Paddy's home on several occasions with his sister, Susan, and had always felt welcomed there. Paddy's siblings shared the same striking features: ginger hair, freckles, and fair skin.

I held a deep affection for Paddy's mother. She possessed a genuine, down-to-earth demeanour and had always treated me with kindness whenever we crossed paths. Her nurturing instincts kicked in effortlessly: ensuring that I was well-fed and taking a keen interest in my well-being. What's more, she had a knack for offering sensible, practical advice, precisely what I needed at that moment. I often expressed to Paddy how fortunate he was to have such a caring mother. I would have given anything to have someone like her in my life.

"Paddy, that'd be great, but I wouldn't want to get ye all in trouble for hiding me from the police," I responded. Paddy dashed off home regardless to ask his parents, and I started to feel more optimistic about my prospects.

We hung around in the cafe for another cup of tea. George and I sat and discussed where I might find a live-in job. He suggested I try all the big posh houses. I couldn't help but notice that he didn't take his eyes off me. It was evident that he wanted me to stay around Omagh. I would have like that too but, although it was nice to have some friends, he made me feel slightly uneasy. Soon, Paddy returned out of breath but with a big smile. He must have run the whole way there and back.

"My ma said yeah, you're welcome to stay for as long as ye need, and ye can stay on the couch. She said to come back with me at dinnertime this evening. When I told her about your auntie, she called her a name I won't repeat!"

"Oh, that's grand; thanks, Paddy. I'll start looking for a job tomorrow. I need to make a plan and get up nice and early in the morning."

Paddy's family warmly welcomed me into their home, where they greeted me with open arms and served up a delicious bowl of homemade Irish stew. They had already prepared a cosy sleeping arrangement on the couch for me. Throughout the evening, Paddy stayed by my side until the early hours of the morning, teaching me card games and doing his best to keep my mind occupied. It felt surreal to be in the company of a caring and supportive family, one that refused to let me fend for myself on the streets. Their kindness and generosity far surpassed anything I had ever experienced from my own family.

As I reflected on why Paddy's family was going out of their way to help me when no one else would, I was overcome with a flood of emotions. The contrast between their compassion and the indifference of my own family left me feeling grateful yet heartbroken.

In the morning, Paddy's mother, Mrs Kerr, brought in a mug of tea to help wake me up. "Thanks, I'll be up in a wee minute."

"Ye don't need to be getting up yet, Frances. I'm just getting this lot ready for school." Paddy's brothers and sisters were already dressed and having breakfast in the kitchen. They all seemed happy to have me stay. Before they left, they each found time to sit and chat with me. He had two younger brothers and two siters, one older and one younger.

As soon as they left, I was up, washed and dressed. "I'm off now to see if I can find some work."

"Good luck, Frances," Mrs Kerr shouted from the kitchen."

"Sure, I'll come with ye, Frances," Paddy jumped out of his chair and followed me.

"Ye could find yourself a wee job too, son," shouted his mother, but Paddy didn't answer. Instead, he banged the door shut behind us and rushed me along the road, grinning. He was in no hurry to find work.

"When I find a job," said Paddy, "It must be right for me, something I don't mind getting out of bed for. I won't be going just to take any old job and make myself miserable."

I understood what he was saying. Unfortunately, I couldn't afford the luxury of thinking that way. I had to find work, and soon, or there would be consequences. That said, the next job I got had to be better than my last job. I wasn't afraid of hard work, but it was apparent that Mrs Quinn wanted a slave. I needed a position where I was treated fairly, allowing me some time for myself.

We walked for a while, joking and laughing but taking shortcuts that kept us away from the main road. I didn't want to be spotted by the police as heading out of town. We headed to where Paddy said the posh houses were. The houses here were well spaced out with large, well-kept gardens. Paddy waited for me on the road and looked out for the police while I went to the doors and inquired about work.

So far, I'd had no luck. It was now one o'clock, and we decided it was time for a break. We walked back into town to the Rex cafe and ordered tea and chips. I sat there worrying that I mightn't find any work while Paddy thought about where to try next. Then, I wondered if anybody was looking for me here yet. I felt sure my Aunty Mary would have phoned the nuns as soon as I'd left her house. She wouldn't want me hanging around in Omagh, job or no job. I was starting to feel desperate, and my mood was very low.

"Wait a wee minute; I'll be back before ye know it," Paddy said and dashed out of the cafe.

He was gone for about ten minutes before returning with George and a newspaper. They ordered a mug of tea for each of us, to justify sitting there and taking up seats. George opened the newspaper onto the table, hoping I might find a job there. We all huddled around to have a look. Unfortunately, there didn't appear to be anything for someone unqualified and without references.

I wasn't prepared to give up yet, so we decided to try some more homes. We finished our tea and set out in a new direction. We must have walked for miles, with me knocking on every promising door, only to be told they didn't need anyone. By now, we were all starting to feel fed up and tired.

"Should we head back home and try again tomorrow, Frances?' Paddy suggested. It was getting late, and his mother would soon have his dinner ready. Paddy was always thinking about his stomach, so we decided to head on back.

On the way, we passed an imposing white house on a hill. It looked amazing. I could see a swimming pool outside. I'd never seen a place with a swimming pool, and I stopped on the road, gazing up at it and wondering what it would be like to live in a house like that.

"That's Doctor McMullan's house. He's me doctor, and he is a nice bloke. Ye can try knocking there if ye want," George suggested.

I didn't hold out much hope. Anyone who owned a house like that would probably have all the staff they needed, but I decided to try it anyway. I felt nervous as I approached the house and crossed my fingers tight before I knocked. A tall, slim, middle-aged lady with blond hair tied back into a high ponytail answered the door. The sound of children playing and laughing rang through the house. I explained to her that I was looking for work and she was telling me that they didn't need anyone when a man came to the door.

He looked at me and then asked me to come in momentarily. He had a kind face, a warm, gentle manner, and a thoughtful expression. He was tall, although most people appeared tall to me as I was short for my age, at just four and a half feet. I'd hoped I still had a little growing to do as I was still only fifteen years old.

"I'm Doctor McMullan," he said as he guided me to a sitting room. "Did someone send ye here to find work," he inquired.

"No. I've just got to find a job. I've been knocking on doors all day but haven't been too lucky yet. I was just about to give up for the day and try again tomorrow when I spotted your house up here."

He told me how impressed he was that someone as young as me would face this amount of trouble to find work. When he asked where my parents lived, I explained that I had grown up in a convent and that if I couldn't find a job, I would have to return to it.

I felt immediately at ease with the doctor, which was unusual. I tended not to trust people, and typically, it would take me much longer to open up to someone. It wasn't long before I was telling him about my last job and the abuse I'd suffered from the nuns. He listened intently, and I could tell he was deeply shocked and moved. He passed a clean handkerchief to me and told me to keep it. It seemed clear to him that my tears were about to start flowing.

Eventually, when I'd answered all his questions, he excused himself to make a phone call. I could hear him say something about 'tomorrow morning' and assumed it was a personal call. On his return, he smiled with pleasure and announced that some friends of his were looking for a nanny. I was overjoyed and relieved this was just what I needed. The job was a living-in position as a nanny for a solicitor's family. It sounded promising, and I began to feel excited and relieved.

"Well, now that's settled, Frances. If you can be here at eight-thirty in the morning, then I'll drive you to the McConnell's home and introduce you to the family. Cheer up, ye have a new friend now and I will not let ye down, Frances, so don't ye be worrying yourself," he said.

It was bizarre, we'd known each other for just a few minutes but I felt I'd known him much longer. I had made a real friend. "Thank you, doctor." I smiled up at him. "I'll be here in the morning."

At the front door, I said goodbye, feeling a lot happier. When I caught up with Paddy and George and told them about my appointment with Mr and Mrs McConnell, they were excited for me and delighted that I would be staying in Omagh. While walking back, Paddy said it might be Mr David McConnell, the solicitor. "Ye'd be so lucky to get that job, Frances. I bet they live in a posh house."

When we arrived at Paddy's house, his family were all pleased for me. George said his goodbyes and went back home for dinner.

I was excited as we sat down to dinner with Paddy's family. Mrs Kerr had made mashed potatoes, cabbage, sausages and gravy. It was a tasty meal, and I enjoyed every bite. All that walking had undoubtedly given me an appetite. After dinner, I helped with the dishes. Mrs Kerr told me I could have a bath and that she'd sort my clothes out so I would look presentable in the morning. I thanked her again for her hospitality and enjoyed a long soak once the younger children were in bed.

It was hard to believe, but it seemed as though my luck was finally changing. If I managed to get this job and phone the nuns to sort things out, then that would stop anyone from looking for me. I sat down and started polishing my shoes, ready for the morning. I was thrilled that everything finally seemed to be going my way. I was looking forward to meeting the doctor again and hoped Mr and Mrs McConnell were as charming and friendly as he was. I felt overwhelmed by how it was all working out and optimistic about my interview in the morning.

Later, when Paddy asked if I wanted to play cards with him, I jumped at the chance to get some practice in, always hoping, one day, to be as good as he was. We played for hours. It took my mind off thinking about my interview, but eventually, at about midnight, Mrs Kerr came in.

"Come on, Paddy, best let Frances get some rest for her interview in the morning."

I felt safe in Paddy's home as I lay down on the couch. I was confident that no one would be looking for me here as I fell into a deep sleep.

The next morning, I was up early and ready to leave by seven-thirty. I wanted to be on time. It was Saturday, and most of Paddy's family were still in bed. Paddy's dad was up making his wife a cup of tea to take to her in bed. Then, Paddy arrived downstairs rubbing his eyes, still looking half-asleep.

"Will ye give me a wee minute, and I'll walk there with ye, Frances. Ye have plenty of time yet," he said, pouring himself some tea from the pot.

"Okay, Paddy, but be quick," I was anxious and didn't want to be late. Although having his company along the road would be great, I wanted to leave a good impression. Mr Kerr laughed at my eagerness.

"Ye look very smart, Frances, and don't worry, Paddy will get ye there on time. I'm sure ye'll get the job all right, but good luck anyway."

We arrived at Doctor McMullan's house ten minutes early. Paddy waited with me for a while, then wished me luck and returned home.

After a few deep breaths, I knocked on the door. The doctor answered almost immediately and told me it was nice to see that I was punctual. It was good to see his friendly face again, and it made me feel even more positive about my interview.

We drove into the town, over a large bridge, and onto Mountjoy Road before finally stopping outside a large three-story house. The big white front door was close to the footpath, and I counted twelve windows at the front, including two that jutted out from the roof. There was no garden at the front, just a long, low wall with a gate at one end leading to the front door. To the side of the house was a solid wooden gate and a tall garden wall. In contrast to the Quinn's house, everything looked in perfect order.

As we approached, the front door opened and we were greeted by a beautifully groomed and well-dressed lady with dark hair and a fair complexion. The doctor introduced me to Mrs McConnell, who seemed very welcoming.

"Come on in," she said, shaking the doctor's hand.

Once inside, I was amazed at how magnificent everything looked. We were shown into one of the two sitting rooms. Mrs McConnell told us that her husband would join us shortly and then left to organise some tea. The room was beautifully furnished with wonderfully restored antique furniture. Nothing looked out of place: each piece had been chosen with great care and had been well looked after. The McConnell's had both money and good taste.

Mrs McConnell returned carrying a large silver tray with a matching silver teapot and some beautiful bone china cups and saucers with a floral pattern. Small pieces of cake were arranged decoratively on a matching plate. She placed the tray on the coffee table and asked the doctor if he would mind pouring it while she fetched her husband. The doctor took pleasure in pouring the tea and, unlike me, seemed quite at home in these surroundings. I guessed that he had socialised here on many occasions. He handed the first cup to me and told me to help myself to sugar and milk.

A few minutes later, Mrs McConnell returned with her husband, a distinguished-looking man whose mere presence commanded respect. He was tall and well-built, with short, brown hair greying a little on the sides.

"I'm pleased to meet with you, Frances," he said politely. He shook my hand and then turned to shake hands with the doctor. They sat down, and Doctor McMullan started the conversation by telling them I'd turned up at his house looking for work. He explained my circumstances with the convent, which I appreciated as it saved me from having to go through it all again. When Mrs McConnell asked if I liked being around children, I told her I loved being with them. For the next half hour or so, I answered their questions and was overjoyed when Mr McConnell said they would love for me to come and work for them and asked if I could start tomorrow morning.

He smiled when I told him I could and asked me to arrive by six o'clock tonight. "We'll get you settled into your room and show you around. You can meet the children before they go off to bed."

As I left the house with the doctor, I felt like I was in a dream and scarcely heard him talking to me.

"Frances, jump in, and I'll give you a lift. Where are ye going?"

"Thank you, doctor. Up the Derry Road, please."

On the way to Paddy's, he told me that I'd made a good impression. I couldn't be happier. I had found a job with a lovely family and was confident that I would be treated very well.

"I will pop in, now and then, to see how you're getting on." Doctor McMullen said when he dropped me off. I couldn't thank him enough for all his help.

"Frances, please take good care of yourself," he said, then drove off.

I arrived at Paddy's house with a beaming smile on my face. The Kerr family were very excited and happy for me. Mrs Kerr hugged me tightly. "Well done, Frances, you can phone those nuns now and tell them that ye have another job," she said, then offered to make me a cheese and ham sandwich and a large mug of tea. I felt the happiest I had ever felt in my life.

I thought I'd better do as she said. I needed to get it done and out of the way, so Paddy and I strolled to the telephone box at the top of the road. I got through to the convent and spoke to Sister Kevin. At first, she wasn't too happy with me for running off like that and said they'd had to inform the police. However, she calmed down when I told her I had found another job. I gave her the details, and she was much happier when I told her that the family was Catholic, and that Mr McConnell was a solicitor. It was a massive weight off my mind: not having to worry about the police searching for me or being sent back to the convent. Before I finished the call, I asked Sister Kevin if she would tell Sinead that I was thinking about her and would visit her in a few weeks, and she said she would.

Back at the house, I played more cards with Paddy and his brother Sean. Paddy's mother washed and pressed my clothes and polished my shoes again to a great shine. Everything was ready for my new life, and it was an exciting time. The rest of the day passed quickly, and soon, it was time to return to the McConnell's. I wondered what it would be like living with them. They seemed so lovely that I was quite looking forward to finding out.

Paddy offered to walk with me again. There wasn't much to do around Omagh, and he loved any excuse to get out and about. Although he was delighted for me, he said he would miss having me around. "Don't worry, Paddy, I'll still come and see ye. I'm just down the road, and Mr McConnell said I would be getting time off in the evenings and a day off on Wednesdays and Sundays. Just don't go chasing me with any more worms." We laughed at the thought of it.

At precisely six o'clock, I rang the doorbell, and Mr McConnell greeted me warmly, ushering me inside. His family was out, but he assured me they would return shortly. In the meantime, he led me up to my room on the attic floor of the house.

As I stepped into the space, I was immediately struck by its beauty. The walls, bedspread, and carpet were all adorned in shades of soothing blue, creating a tranquil atmosphere. An elegant blue lamp sat on bedside table, and beside the bed was a plush white rug with a delicate blue pattern running through it. Opposite the door stood a pristine single-divan bed. Three exquisite pieces of matching mahogany furniture: a spacious wardrobe, a dainty table, and a stunning dressing table completed the main furnishings. A cosy chair with a blue velvet seat sat invitingly in front of the dressing table, offering a perfect spot for quiet reflection. The window was set into the roof and bathed the room in natural light.

As I took in the sight of my new surroundings, I could scarcely believe that such a magnificent room was now mine to call home.

I put my small case down beside the bed. It looked shabby and old - I would hide it later when I was alone. I loved it all so much. It was hard to believe this was where I would sleep tonight.

Mr McConnell then preceded to give me a tour of the rest of the house, and I was awestruck by its grandeur.

The top floor boasted several very tastefully furnished guest rooms and bathrooms. On the first floor, I marvelled at colourful nursery, the beautifully appointed children's bedrooms plus two luxurious family bathrooms. Mr and Mrs McConnell's bedroom was a sight to behold, complete with an en-suite bathroom featuring a sunken bath accessed by steps; I had never seen anything quite like it.

Descending to the ground floor was a well-appointed library and a large children's playroom - brimming with colour and stimulation. The dining room, kitchen, and utility room were meticulously organised and equipped, reflecting the utmost attention to detail, and a large reception room provided a welcoming space for guests. Finally, I was taken aback by the presence of a tiny chapel, where Mr McConnell's brother, a priest, would conduct mass during his visits.

Each room was impeccably decorated and furnished in a way that surpassed anything I had ever seen. It was difficult to fathom that I could be so fortunate as to live in such a magnificent place. I found myself falling in love with it more with each passing moment.

Returning to the kitchen, Mr McConnell kindly suggested that we enjoy a cup of tea while awaiting the return of the family, a gesture that further underscored the warmth and hospitality that permeated every corner of the house.

As I sat at the kitchen table, observing Mr McConnell, a sense of unease washed over me. He appeared somewhat out of place, and I felt that the task of making tea for someone like me was beneath him. I couldn't shake the feeling that I should be the one serving him, not the other way around.

Despite my discomfort, Mr McConnell proceeded to outline my duties and the house rules as we sipped our tea. He explained that Susan, the cleaner, was responsible for all the housework and ironing, ensuring that the home remained in impeccable condition. Additionally, Nurse McGowan tended to the needs of the new baby just as she had cared for the older children, all six of them. I learned that I would not be involved with the baby until Nurse McGowan departed, which typically occurred when the child reached eight months of age.

My responsibilities revolved solely around caring for the other children in the household. Each morning, my duties began with assisting the younger ones in getting washed, dressed, and fed, a task I approached with gratitude, especially considering the reprieve from porridge. Instead, the children were given the freedom to choose their preferred cereal, which I would then serve into their bowls. Jugs of milk or cream, along with a sugar bowl, were placed on the table for their convenience, making the breakfast routine a straightforward affair.

Ensuring the older children were prepared for school on time was also part of my morning routine. I was to make certain they were ready for Mrs McConnell, who drove them to their school. Throughout the rest of the day, my focus shifted to tending to the needs of the younger children, which included preparing their meals, assisting them with feeding themselves, and keeping them entertained with games and stories.

My duties continued until six o'clock in the evening, culminating with bathing the children and dressing them in their pyjamas for bedtime. It was a routine that brought structure and purpose to my days, and I approached each task with dedication and care.

During the evenings, I was free to pursue my own interests and socialise, provided I returned home before ten-thirty when Mr McConnell secured the house for the night. Wednesdays and Sundays, which I would grow to cherish, were designated as my days off, offering a welcome break from my duties.

However, there were two important rules that I was expected to adhere to: alcohol was strictly prohibited within the confines of the home, a rule rooted in Mr McConnell's firsthand observations of lives ravaged by its influence. Additionally, if I wished to smoke, I was required to do so outside in the garden, respecting the household's preference for a smoke-free environment.

In exchange for my services, I would receive a weekly wage of three pounds and ten shillings—a generous compensation that underscored the value placed on my contributions. Every aspect of the job seemed ideal, and I eagerly anticipated the opportunity to meet and care for the children under my charge. My heart swelled with joy at the prospect of embarking on this new chapter of my life.

"Ah, that'll be them now," said Mr McConnell as he got up to answer the door.

Soon, the sound of children talking and laughing rang throughout the home, and it was as if suddenly the place had come to life. "Come and meet Frances. She is going to be your new nanny," I heard Mr McConnell say.

As the children trailed behind their parents into the kitchen, I couldn't help but notice their striking good looks, a trait undoubtedly inherited from their parents. Mrs McConnell beamed with pride as she introduced each of them in turn.

First was David, the eldest at ten years old, bearing his father's name. Following closely behind was Eileen, a nine-year-old girl named after her beloved mother, reflecting the deep bond between parent and child.

Next in line was Roman, approaching his eighth birthday, followed by Robert, a lively six-year-old brimming with energy and enthusiasm. Sean, at the tender age of four, exuded a sense of curiosity and wonder, while two-year-old Patrick completed the lineup, his chubby features eliciting smiles from all who saw him.

As I gazed upon the McConnell children, I couldn't help but feel a sense of warmth and anticipation, eager to embark on this new journey of caring for and nurturing these delightful young children.

Mrs McConnell had just finished her introduction when the nurse entered with the baby, Coleen. "Hello, Frances, pleased to meet you. I'm sure we'll get along just grand." She spoke with a soft, warm southern Irish accent, wore a broad smile and was dressed in an immaculate nurse's uniform. She had grey permed hair and wore thick glasses. I guessed she was probably in her early sixties.

Everything about the home seemed perfect: the house, the children, the McConnell's and my excellent room. It would take some time to sink in, but I was confident I would be happy living and working for this wonderful family.

Over the next eight months, I settled into living in the McConnell household. Life was wonderful, and I was finally thriving. My confidence in myself and my future was slowly developing, and I could not imagine being any happier. Nurse McGowan had left, and I was now helping Mrs McConnell look after the baby. I could hardly believe I was getting paid to live in that lovely house and to spend my time doing what I enjoyed most: looking after those children. It was a joy, and my life was great.

When the weather was good, we would spend time in the nearby park with a picnic lunch, and I would watch the children play and laugh without a care. It was hard for me not to envy their childhood a little. Not that I wished their lives were any different. I was happy for them but sad for my sisters and myself.

Whenever I thought about our childhood, it was always painful. Sometimes, I would find myself crying at the most awkward times. When the children or other people were around, I would try to find a way of covering it up: pretending to have something in my eye or that my hay fever was bad.

The McConnell's were kind to me. Mrs McConnell would buy me gifts of clothes or perfume. When she discovered that I was making up stories for the children, because I couldn't read their books, she paid for me to take reading lessons at evening classes in the tech college. I attended a few times but felt very embarrassed. Trying to read simple children's books in front of others made me feel stupid. It was a slow process, but with a little help from others and a lot of determination, I eventually taught myself to read.

I'd visited Sinead several times, and, on my last visit, she told me that she thought she might get released soon. One of the nuns had let it slip, but she wasn't sure when. I was excited for her and told her to behave and not mess up her chances. I told her where I worked and asked her to come and find me or to let me know where she was. Sinead was tall and tanned with long blond hair and big brown eyes. I thought she could probably be a model one day. She would have looked great, even while wearing a bin liner.

I became very fond of the children, especially Patrick, who was now almost three. I had spent most of my time with him, as the others were at school or nursery, and a strong bond had developed between us. I loved him being around me: he was adorable and cuddly. When he tried to say my name, he would pronounce it as Sess, and I would laugh at how funny it sounded.

On my days off, he would get upset when I left him. I hated seeing him upset, so I started taking him with me on Wednesdays. I didn't want the others to feel he was my favourite, so I gave them turns to come out with me on Sundays.

Usually, I would spend my days off going into town. Sometimes, I'd call in to see Paddy's family. I would get whichever child was with me back to the house by five o'clock, and then have the evening to myself. In the evenings' Paddy and George would sometimes wait for me to come out, and we would hang out together around the cafe or just walk about town. There wasn't much else to do, and I had no one else to go out with.

It soon became obvious that George didn't want Paddy to hang around with us. He always seemed to be trying to make up any excuse to get rid of him, making him feel that he was in the way. I liked Paddy. He had a wicked sense of humour and made me laugh. He was also very genuine, and he knew I didn't think he was in the way: we were friends. I was pleased he wasn't allowing George to bully him and push him out.

One sunny morning, Mrs McConnell called me into the library for a chat. She informed me that the family was going on holiday in a few weeks. They owned a holiday home in Canada and flew over twice a year. The children adored being there, and she invited me to accompany them. It was a wonderful gesture, and I was surprised they would invite me to go. She said she would understand if I wanted to remain and asked me to consider it. Nurse McGowan would return to stay with baby Coleen and look after the house. Also, Susan would be in daily to do a thorough deep clean while they were gone. It was my choice if I wanted to go or not.

I appreciated her invitation and desperately wanted to accept this fantastic offer. However, now, the brainwashing from my past kicked in. Suddenly, I could hear sister Thomas's voice saying, "You're from the gutter, Reilly. You need to know your place. You're not deserving of this." I could hear her voice spinning around and around in my head on a perpetual loop, and I suddenly felt nauseous and uncomfortable. Perhaps, I thought, Mrs McConnell was inviting me out of pity, and I would be a burden on the family. Agonising over it, I ached to be normal like other people. My face was flushed, and I didn't know how to respond. She saw that I was struggling with my decision and asked me to consider it. My wages would still be paid either way, she assured me.

The following day, I gave the holiday idea much thought and finally decided to stay at the house. The nurse and Susan would be good company: I got on well with them both and thought that having this big house all to ourselves would be the perfect time to get to know each other better. Also, I didn't want to have to admit the impact that convent life had had on me: I wasn't ready yet to leave the comfort and security of these surroundings.

That evening, I told Mrs McConnell that I would prefer to stay. She looked as though she understood. I think she assumed that I would feel more comfortable in the company of the staff.

Once I'd made my decision, everything felt different, and I was filled with excitement and anticipation. Mr and Mrs McConnell were busier than usual, organising the holiday arrangements and tying up urgent business matters, and the children were busy picking out the toys and books they wished to take with them. I had fun helping them pack their toys, books, and clothes. The older children constantly sang, "We're all going on a summer holiday." There was a contagious holiday buzz about the house.

Departure day soon arrived, and the children found it hard to contain their excitement over breakfast. The older children said they would bring me back a present. They chattered incessantly about everything they'd done on their last holiday and the things they were hoping to do this time. Usually, the mornings were much more relaxed and quieter. Their parents heard all the chatter and laughing and joined us in the kitchen. Mr McConnell put on a record of "Chitty-Chitty-Bang-Bang," quite loudly, and they all sang along. They would have a great time, I was sure, and I was happy for them. After breakfast, I helped the children bathe and prepare for their journey.

The nurse and Susan arrived, and soon we were waving the McConnell's off. As soon as they'd left, the house seemed more imposing and emptier and echoed in their absence. Still trying to figure out what to do now that the children were no longer in the house, we returned to the kitchen and attempted to adjust to the change in atmosphere. Susan made a pot of tea and put some biscuits on a plate, and we all sat down for a wee break. Nurse McGowan gulped her tea and went to the nursery to check on Coleen, leaving Susan and me to chat. It was a beautiful sunny day, so we poured another cup of tea and took it into the garden.

Sitting on the grass and smoking a cigarette, it felt peaceful and relaxing. As soon as the family had gone, I had changed the record on the record player for one of my own, and the music of Dave Edmond's drifted out through the open window of the kitchen. It was an excellent way to adjust, and we ended up smoking quite a few cigarettes as we got to know each other better.

Now that the children had gone, I had nothing to do. Mrs McConnell had left me strict instructions to have a break and relax. It was glorious: sitting, enjoying the sunshine in this fantastic garden with the mixed scent of sweet peas and roses wafting around in the air. It was the closest I'd been to what I imagined was paradise.

Susan had two weeks to get the house cleaned from top to bottom. She usually only worked four days a week but was delighted to get in every day for the overtime. She confided in me that she lived alone in a small flat but was planning to get married next year, so the extra money would be extremely helpful.

She had many wedding arrangements already ticked off her list, but there was still much to do to make it her dream day. I enjoyed Susan's company, but we rarely had time to chat, so it was wonderful having this time together. She was a real down-to-earth, straight-arrow who never cut corners with any job she worked on, earning every penny the McConnell's paid her.

I confided in her a few things about my childhood: how life had been for my sisters and me growing up in care with the nuns and priests. A devout Catholic and compassionate individual, she found my story hard to comprehend. She said she would never be able to tell her family what the nuns had done because they would not believe a word of it. She didn't want to consider it, but, when she focused on what I was saying, she knew that I was being truthful.

I deliberately didn't reveal too much, knowing how much she was struggling to absorb what I was telling her. However, it was important to me that she believed what I was telling her, and I was grateful to her for that. Too many people simply didn't want to hear and were unwilling to believe anything negative about the Catholic church.

When she got up to start on her work, I got stuck in too. She didn't ask, but I wanted to help as it allowed us to talk a bit more. Also, with the extra help, she could afford to take a few more breaks.

As the days progressed, she showed an increasing interest in my life at the convent, and I trusted her with some more revelations. The empathy showed on her face which sometimes distorted with disgust and contempt at what she was hearing. When she commented on how 'matter of fact' I was when normalising these atrocities, it made me reflect on just how abnormal they were. However, to my sisters and me, and to too many others, this had been our normality.

"You have to complain to someone, Frances!" she insisted.

Before she suggested anything else, I insisted to her that it could worsen things. "Remember, ye said your parents wouldn't believe ye, Susan. Well, if they wouldn't believe you then no one would believe me!"

I explained to Susan that I had told my story to Bernadette Devlin, the Catholic MP for Cookstown, the last time I ran away. "I told her everything!" I explained. "And I'm still waiting to hear back from her." Tears welled up in my eyes with the memory of that night. I hated it when that happened, but I couldn't control it.

We smoked many cigarettes and drank a load of tea but completed much housework over the next few weeks. Despite all the work, I also found time to relax and go into town.

The days passed quickly, and soon we were saying "They'll be back tomorrow." And, with no one about to mess it up, the house looked splendid. I imagined the family being extremely pleased with all of it when they returned. The windows were so clean that there appeared to be no glass in the frames. The only dust seen was on the tall rubber plant in the entrance hall. I thought I would try to be helpful and clean it.

Susan explained, "I don't usually tend to the plant, Frances. It's so big that it's hard to reach most of it. Mr McConnell does it now and then; he uses a ladder, but I'm unsure where he keeps it." Susan sounded nervous, worried I might have an accident, but I reassured her that I would be careful. It did look like it would be a challenging job to tackle, but I thought it would be worth it when it was done. It would be a pleasant surprise for the McConnell family when they returned.

It took me most of the afternoon; at times, I had been hanging dangerously off the railing. When I stood back and saw the difference it made to the plant, I thought I'd done a fantastic job, but I certainly wouldn't want to do it again. For now, though, it looked worth all the effort. I gazed proudly at it, hoping the family would appreciate my effort.

When Nurse McGowan came to call me for a tea break. She was very impressed and called Susan to come and have a look. "That's amazing, Frances. I've never seen that plant looking so good," she said.

"Yeah, that's a grand job, Frances," Susan agreed.

Back in the kitchen, Susan announced that all her work was finished. "That's it then; the house is ready for them to come home." Nurse McGowan made some tea and suggested that we sit a while and chat, then take a nice walk in the park with baby Coleen. The weather was pleasantly warm, and a brisk walk was an excellent idea to pass the time. It had been a pleasurable but very different experience with the McConnell family away, but I had missed the children and would be glad to see them back home.

The McConnell's returned home in high spirits. Mr and Mrs McConnell were delighted with how everything looked and told Susan she'd done a grand job. Mr McConnell immediately noticed the plant, and Susan told him I had cleaned it.

"You must have been very bored, Frances," he said. "We were going to get rid of this old thing to a hotel or old people's home, as it's grown too big now. We might have to hang on to it for a while longer now that it's looking this good." I was thrilled that my efforts had been appreciated.

The children couldn't wait to tell me all about their holiday. They'd all had a great time. After they ran off to see Coleen in the nursery, they returned with gifts for Nurse McGowan, Susan, and myself. I received a tin of toffees from the children and a lovely yellow and white blouse from Mr and Mrs McConnell. Susan got an ornament for her flat, and the nurse got a beautiful gift box of bath salts, talcum powder, and soaps. It was good to have the McConnell's back home and to hear children in the house once again. However, I was going to miss my long smoke breaks and chats with Susan.

That evening, I wore my new blouse with a skirt that Mrs McConnell had bought for my birthday a few months earlier. When I tidied my hair and checked my appearance in the mirror, I hardly recognised myself as the same person who'd grown up in the orphanage. Fortunately, the emotional scars didn't show, and I looked like any typical sixteen-year-old teenager getting ready to go out for the evening. I said goodnight to the children and left to see if Paddy and George were waiting for me up the road.

When I met them, they were talking about the Troubles again. The riots had become more frequent and intense, and people had started making petrol bombs in their gardens, ready for use. Fortunately, Omagh had been quiet compared to Belfast and Derry, but the Troubles were now affecting everyone. Armed soldiers and military checkpoints had become a regular feature, and wherever you went, there was the persistent feeling that you were never safe from the bombings and shootings.

Paddy said it wouldn't be too long before it would be us trying to defend ourselves. I didn't like to think about that, so I didn't follow the news, but people always discussed it. It was hard to escape it wherever you went: shops, cafes, and on the street. It was hard for people not to speculate about what would happen next.

While I often tried to steer the conversation toward lighter subjects, I found myself hesitating, unwilling to risk triggering George's habit of boring us with yet more tales of Bruce Lee or with his comical attempts at mimicking his martial arts idol.

It wasn't that I disliked Bruce Lee. I admired the man's talent and charisma, but George's relentless obsession with emulating him had begun to wear thin. His clumsy attempts at mimicking Bruce Lee, often at Paddy's expense, had grown tiresome. I found myself bracing for yet another round of his antics and whenever the topic arose.

Later, as we sat in the cafe, enjoying a simple meal of chips and coke, I attempted to steer the conversation away from the Troubles, sharing anecdotes about my job and the day-to-day happenings in the McConnell household, but my efforts were quickly overshadowed by the looming spectre of the Troubles.

Crazy About Bruce Lee

One evening, as I ventured out of the house, scanning the familiar streets for any sign of the boys, I was surprised to find George standing alone. He explained that Paddy was elsewhere, off with his father for the time being. With no other plans in sight, we made our way to the Rex cafe, where we settled in and ordered our usual fare of chips and coke.

Seated together, George's fervour for Bruce Lee quickly became evident, his admiration for the martial arts legend spilling forth in animated tales of Bruce's legendary exploits. His impassioned discussions frequently turned into impromptu demonstrations of Kung Fu manoeuvres, drawing curious gazes from bystanders. I found their attention somewhat discomforting.

While George seemed convinced that channelling Bruce Lee's prowess lent him an air of strength and charisma, I couldn't shake the feeling of unease at being the unwitting audience to his theatrics.

Behind George's back, his friends would share amused whispers about his obsession with Bruce Lee and his seemingly unattainable aspiration to emulate the martial arts legend. While they found humour in his earnest attempts, I couldn't shake the feeling that George's ambitions far outstripped his abilities. And yet, despite the odds stacked against him, he persisted in his pursuit of his idol, undeterred by the scepticism of others.

It wasn't that I harboured any ill will toward George, but I always felt more comfortable when we were around others. There was always a certain level of unease that lingered between us, a discomfort born from his overt confidence in proclaiming his intentions to marry me one day, a notion that, as far as I was concerned, seemed more fantasy than reality. As far as I was concerned, that was never going to happen.

While I was still in the convent, he once turned up unexpectedly one Sunday afternoon, boldly declaring to the nuns that he was my boyfriend. I was caught off guard and felt incredibly embarrassed in front of the other girls and the nuns. My face flushed with heat, and I could only imagine how red it must have appeared. Despite the awkwardness of the situation, the nuns granted him twenty minutes to see me, considering the distance he had travelled.

"What are ye doing here, George?" I'd asked him. "Ye do know that I'll probably be in trouble now, even though I've done nothing wrong. And they may not be too keen on letting me return to my aunt's again!"

I might have felt flattered by his attention if I hadn't been so shy of boys unless they only wanted to be friends. I hadn't been around boys much, and I'd never had a boyfriend. I wasn't sure that I was ready for one.

Sinead told me she thought he had a nerve to say he was my boyfriend. "He's just trying to claim you like you're his possession. He's being creepy." Sinead had never liked or trusted George.

Later, when I suggested calling in to see if Paddy was home, George said we should take a shortcut over the old railway line. As we walked along, he talked about Bruce Lee and bodybuilding. I was so bored of that conversation, but he continued trying to impress me. George told me that if he ever had a son, he would call him after Bruce Lee. I laughed out loud at him and joked that Bruce wasn't a nice name for a baby. It was more like the name you gave to a bulldog or a boxer. He got offended by what I'd said, so I tried to make things better.

"Ye could name him Lee. That's a good name," I suggested.

"Yeah, I like that. Maybe I could name him Bruce Lee, but just call him Lee," he said, as though he needed to decide immediately.

It was pitch black and quite spooky as we walked along the old railway line. George knew the way very well as he'd grown up playing along it, and he told me that he'd sometimes taken his brother's motorbike for a ride on it.

"Hold on to my arm, or ye might trip over something," he suggested.

"We'll be at Paddy's in about ten minutes." I held onto the arm of his jacket, which made me feel safer. I didn't like that I couldn't see a thing and wished we were near the road again.

We walked on a bit further before George stopped to light two cigarettes, giving me one. He seemed to know the exact place we had stopped. George struck another match to highlight how far away we were from the grassy bank. "Let's sit here for a minute and smoke our fags," he said, helping me find my bearings.

"Okay, George, but let's get going after we've smoked these. This place gives me the creeps."

"Sure, you'll be okay with me here. If anybody jumps out, I can handle myself. Don't worry about that." he boasted.

I had no doubt he could fight. Paddy had told me George had done boxing at school and was quite good at it. I didn't know how good he was, but I couldn't help thinking he'd probably try Kung Fu on them, and then we'd be in big trouble. Fortunately, we sat there undisturbed until we stubbed out our cigarettes on the ground. Then, George frightened me by jumping up and shouting, "Did ye hear that?"

"No, what was it?" I whispered, terrified. George sat beside me, put his arm around me, and told me to be quiet.

I was terrified but did as he asked, listening intently for anyone who might be out there. There wasn't a sound, and after a few minutes or so, I wondered if George was playing games with me.

"I don't hear anything, George. Let's just go," Unfortunately, George had other things on his mind and leaned across to kiss me and pushed me back until we were lying on the ground with his total weight on top of me. His hand groped me under my skirt and pulled at my knickers. I tried to struggle from under him, but it only made things worse. He grew more excited and began working on undoing his zip.

"Get off me, George, stop it! We need to be going now." But it was too late: he had penetrated me, and memories of childhood abuse flashed through my head and filled my mind. It was over in minutes, and he rolled off and zipped up his jeans. I got to my feet in the dark. I quietly pulled myself together and, given the circumstances, fixed my clothes as quickly as possible.

George lit two cigarettes and casually handed me one. "Hear ye go, Frances, smoke this on the way to Paddy's." I could just about see the glowing tip, and, dazed, I took it.

"I'm not going to Paddy's. I'm going back to the McConnell's house." I snapped.

We walked along in silence until we reached the Derry Road, not far from where George and Paddy lived. The illumination from the streetlights provided a sense of relief as I could now see my surroundings clearly. With a heavy heart, I instructed George to continue his way, and without hesitation, I broke into a run down the Derry Road, desperate to put as much distance between us as possible. As I felt the gap widening between us, I slowed my pace to a walk. Overcome with emotions, tears welled up as I grappled with the betrayal of our friendship, yearning for the safety and comfort of the McConnell household.

Mr McConnell greeted me at the door with a look of surprise and asked if I was all right. "You're not normally home this early, Frances."

"I'm fine, Mr McConnell; I just want an early night." My voice quivered, and I was sure he knew what was wrong.

I crept up to the nearest bathroom to my room, not wanting to disturb anyone, and locked the door behind me.

Lying there in the bath for ages, I was surrounded by soft white bubbles. The hot water felt comforting and healing, like a warm blanket wrapped around me, soothing my troubled mind. I hoped the bath would wash away the memory and dirt, maybe leaving me feeling back to normal after a good night's sleep.

As the water cooled, I started to wash, and it was then that I noticed blood on my flannel. It scared me: it wasn't my time of the month, and I felt sore, worried that George had damaged me in some way. Finding more blood on the towel as I dried myself only added to my confusion and fear. Unsure of what to do, I washed the towel and my underwear, fearing someone might realise what had happened.

Taking them back to my room to dry on the radiator, I couldn't shake off the worry about the blood, but there was nothing more I could do, so I went to bed and tried to sleep. It took a while before I could push away the worries and feelings of that evening, but eventually, I drifted off.

The alarm went off, jolting me out of bed. As I dressed, I noticed, to my relief, that the bleeding had stopped. I still felt awful, but I managed to get ready on time to prepare breakfast for the children. They were still discussing their holiday, and I enjoyed hearing all about it. I had missed them and talking with them now helped take my mind off George. With the children still off school, they asked if we could go to the park, and I happily agreed.

When their mother came downstairs, she thought it was a lovely idea and decided to go too. She suggested we have a little picnic for lunch. As we walked through the front hall, she commented on how nice the plant looked and thanked me for my effort. It felt great to get validation. Anyone who grew up like me needed confirmation now and then.

It was a gorgeous day, and the park was crowded with people who had the same idea of enjoying the weather. Mrs McConnell sat down with Coleen on a blanket in the shade of a tree while I played ball with Patrick. The older children ran off to the swings.

After lunch, I took Patrick over to the swings, and before leaving, we all ran around the park playing a very long game of tag. When we returned to the house, we were hot, sweaty and tired, but it had been a great day. I'd been so busy that I'd barely had time to think. It was just what I needed.

Later that evening, I was helping the younger children take their baths. They liked to jump in two at a time and play with their bath toys for a while before I washed them. As I sat on the chair in their bathroom, watching to make sure they were playing safely, the events of the last evening flooded my mind.

Usually, as soon as the children were bathed and in their pyjamas, I'd be getting ready to go out. However, tonight I felt like going nowhere, but, if I stayed in, Mr and Mrs McConnell would want to know what was wrong. I wondered if Paddy would be waiting for me, and if George would be with him. I wanted to ask Paddy what he'd been doing with his dad last night, which left me alone with George. I wasn't ready to face George yet. I couldn't decide what to do!

When the children were ready for bed, I gathered them around me in the playroom and told them stories. The stories went on for ages and, eventually, Mr McConnell came in and said, "Come on now, they've had enough of your time today, Frances. Don't let this lot keep you. Get yourself off now."

I went to my room and got ready but couldn't bring myself to go out, so I just sat on the bed. I must have been sitting there for about twenty minutes when Mrs McConnell knocked on the door. "Frances, a boy has knocked for you, and I've asked him to wait outside," she said.

"Thank you, Mrs McConnell," I answered through the door. Outside, I could see Paddy and George standing by the garden gate.

"What took ye so long?" asked Paddy while George paced back and forth nervously. He didn't say a word or look at me. Instead, he hung his head as though examining something on the path. I don't think he wanted to be there, but I'm sure he was concerned that, left on our own, I might confide in Paddy.

I told Paddy that the children wanted another story, and he laughed and told me I was too soft with them. "So, where shall we go?" Paddy asked.

"I don't care," I replied.

"It's a lovely day. We could take a wander down by the river," George suggested. Paddy agreed, so we started walking in that direction.

Paddy and George were mucking about, pushing and shoving each other along the way. That suited me fine so long as I didn't have to put up any conversation. When we got to the river, they tried shoving each other into the water. I got the feeling that George was trying to impress me. He failed! He was just annoying me. Whenever I looked at him, I flashed back to the previous night. Usually, I would have been laughing at them for being so childish, but now I just let them get on with it. I was sitting on the grass, in my own little world, pulling up clumps of grass and throwing them in the river when Paddy shouted, "Come on, Frances, we're walking along the river."

When I caught up with them, George was telling Paddy about a Bruce Lee film he'd seen. "Did ye enjoy it, George?" Paddy asked.

"Yeah, it wasn't just good; it was fantastic," George shouted, trying to get me interested in the conversation. Usually, I'd be happy to join in with what they were talking about.

"I am sure Bruce Lee is fantastic," I said sarcastically. That was when Paddy realised, I was in a bad mood.

"What's the matter with ye, Frances? Ye hardly said a word since ye came out." I could tell he was concerned, but before I could say anything, George butted in.

"Sure, she's fine, aren't ye, Frances,"

"Yeah, I'm fine, Paddy. I'm just a bit tired, and I've got a headache, that's all." Paddy looked as though he didn't believe me but said nothing. However, by the time we arrived at the cafe, he was sure something was wrong.

"Have you two fallen out?" he asked as soon as George disappeared to the toilet.

"I don't want to talk about it, Paddy," I told him. "Just leave it at that."

"Yeah, fair enough, but ye can trust me." He assured me he wouldn't tell George if I confided in him.

"I know, Paddy. Thanks."

Back at the McConnell's, I kept telling myself not to think about George. However, he kept creeping back into my mind whenever I tried to sleep. I was angry, but there seemed to be nothing I could do. Over the next few days, I kept myself busy and tried to hide that something was wrong. Playing with the children helped, but suddenly, I would remember and feel as dirty and degraded as I had at the time. I had started bathing in the mornings and evenings, but soap and water weren't enough. I still felt dirty inside.

While I was on a break, having a cup of tea with Susan, Mrs McConnell entered the kitchen. "Frances, what did you use to clean the rubber plant?" she asked.

I assumed she was so impressed that she wanted to try it herself. Smiling proudly, I answered, "Pledge."

"Pledge furniture polish?" she sounded surprised.

"Yes, Mrs McConnell, and there's plenty left in the cupboard," I suggested, trying to be helpful.

She looked at me, her jaw dropped open and then started laughing hysterically. Susan and I started laughing, too, although I wasn't sure why. It was strange to see Mrs McConnell, who was typically very reserved, laughing like that. The laughing continued for a few minutes, and I wondered what was so funny.

When she eventually started to calm down, Susan looked at me in disbelief as Mrs McConnell announced. "Ye don't clean plants with furniture polish, Frances." She was trying not to burst out laughing again. Susan and I followed Mrs McConnell into the hall. There stood the plant, its leaves limp and brown.

"Oh my God, I'm so sorry, Mrs McConnell. I didn't know." I felt foolish, but Mrs McConnell just started laughing again.

"Don't ye worry, Frances, we were going to get rid of it anyway. It had become uncontrollable, and now I have a good excuse to throw it out. Besides, you've given us a good laugh and a funny story to entertain our guests for years." It was good to see her laughing like that, and I was proud to be the reason for it.

Unexpected News

Over the next few weeks, everything appeared to be back to normal. I was getting on well at work and continued meetings with Paddy and George in the evenings. George and I were grudgingly back on speaking terms, although I ensured that he was not able to try anything with me again. He apologised continuously and finally managed to talk me around, somehow. He even made me feel a bit sorry for him, telling me that I made him feel like he did and that a bloke couldn't control those urges.

I suppose that, after all that had happened to me as a child, I was so used to taking the blame that it was almost normal. Also, I wanted to make life easier for everyone, so I tried to pretend it had not happened. I told myself that I would not be caught in a situation like that ever again.

Most of the time, I was coping okay. However, now, and then, I would flashback to that awful night. At times, it was hard to put on an act, and I was sure that someone would realise that something was bothering me. To make matters worse, I had recently started suffering from what I thought might be a bug. It had been going on for a few days now, and I just could not shake it off, which was unusual for me: I was hardly ever poorly.

One morning, I got up and was so ill that I couldn't leave the bathroom. I could hear the children telling their father they hadn't had breakfast because Frances hadn't come down yet. I was about five minutes late and trying hard to be all right. When Mr McConnell called me, I found it impossible to answer.

"Come on, children, I'll get your breakfast. I'm sure Frances will be up soon." I heard him saying to the children.

A few minutes later, Mrs McConnell knocked on the door outside the bathroom. She'd heard me throwing up and wanted to know if I was all right.

"I'll be okay, Mrs McConnell. I'll be down in a minute," I answered.

"Get yourself back to bed, Frances, and I'll bring you a cup of tea," she insisted.

I struggled back into bed, feeling weak and drained. A few minutes later, she returned with a tray bearing a steaming pot of tea and some toast. "Try to eat some breakfast; it might help you feel better," she suggested. gently, placing the tray on the bedside table. As she reached out to feel my forehead, concern etched across her face, she continued, "I'll phone Doctor McMullan and see if he'll come and take a look at you.

Early in the afternoon, Doctor McMullan examined me. However, I was feeling much better by then. Afterwards, he sat on my bed, and we talked for a while. I was always pleased to see him but had never seen him as my doctor. Before leaving, he asked if I would come to his surgery at five o'clock to register with him and have some tests. The surgery was only a few minutes walk from the McConnell's house, and I promised to be there.

"Now don't ye worry, Frances, I'll soon have ye back on your feet," he reassured me.

After he'd gone, Susan popped in to see me with another a cup of tea. I'd been alone most of the day and was pleased to have her company.

"Are ye all right, Frances? What did the doctor say was wrong?"

"He didn't say, but he wants to see me go to the surgery at five for some tests. Susan stayed a while to chat. Everyone was fussing at me, and it felt good knowing they cared. At the surgery, the receptionist gave me some forms to fill in and asked me to sit. When it was my turn, I walked along nervously, looking at the names on the doors, when I saw Doctor McMullan waiting for me.

"Hello, Frances. I'm glad you could make it. Come on in."

Just seeing him there was reassuring he could put people at ease instantly. He took my forms and said he would fill them in for me. Then he sent me off, with a nurse, for a blood and urine test.

Afterwards, he sat me down in his room and told me that he'd ensured that I was his last patient so that he would have plenty of time to spend with me. He made me feel special and deserving of his attention. "We can chat while we wait for a prescription," he suggested. "I know it's annoying, but you'll have to wait a few days for your blood and urine results."

Doctor McMullan filled in my forms: my reading was improving slowly, but I would have struggled to complete it on my own. Then, we discussed my time in the convent and how I was getting on living at the McConnell's. Almost half an hour must have passed before the nurse returned with the prescription.

The next few days dragged by, and I was still feeling unwell. I didn't know what the doctor was testing for, and I prayed to the universe that it was nothing serious. At last, the results were back, and I had an appointment at five o'clock. I arrived there too early, so I paced up and down the path with a cigarette, worrying about what could be wrong with me. Finally, Doctor McMullen came out and asked me to come into the surgery. Once again, I was his last patient. I followed him in and took a seat.

He picked up a sheet of paper from his desk and stared at it as he shook his head and frowned. "This confirms what I've been thinking, Frances. The test shows that you're pregnant. You're going to have a wee baby."

I wasn't sure what he was saying. I didn't know what pregnant meant. Once, when someone in the convent got pregnant, she had been sent away. When she returned, she was forbidden from talking to us about it. When I asked a nun what it meant, I got a hard slap on the face and was told not to be so disgusting, so I never asked again. I had no idea where the baby would come from, but I was pleased to be getting one. I loved babies.

I thought that having a baby of my own would be brilliant. I would have someone to love and who could love me back. I imagined a little girl dressed up in frills, like the doll I'd never owned, but this would be a real baby. As I looked at the doctor excitedly, my thoughts were that I could never put my baby in a convent. "Oh, that's great, doctor. When am I going to get my baby?" I asked him.

"I would think in about seven months. I won't book you into the hospital until you've told the father and are married. It will save you the embarrassment of being booked as a single mother."

I knew what he meant about having a baby without being married. I had heard of a few single mothers that had been treated like lepers: disowned by their friends and families and talked about like they were the worst sort of scum. It can't have been good for them to live like that.

"Do ye know who your baby's father is, Frances?"

"Sure, I haven't had time yet to decide who will be the father. You've only just told me I was getting a baby."

Doctor McMullan looked at me dumbfounded and bewildered. Then he explained that someone must have done something to me and made me pregnant. I thought about what he was saying, but it didn't register immediately what he was trying to say. I still hadn't made any connection between what had happened with George and having a baby. That was just some horrible thing that had happened and that I'd rather forget. I had no idea of the possible consequences and thought I had to pick somebody who would be a great daddy. It must have sounded very naive, but there was no talk of sex or babies in the convent, and with no family or friends to explain things, I had no idea what had happened to me.

"This could take a wee while now," Doctor McMullen said, it sounded like he was talking to himself rather than to me. I was grateful for his patience. We talked and talked until, at last, the penny dropped. George was the daddy, and I would have to go and tell him. Only then could I get booked into the hospital? Now I understood and it terrified me.

The doctor made another appointment and gave me some iron tablets. "You'll have to tell the father as soon as possible. Look after yourself, Frances," he said as I left the surgery.

George had taken a job in the dispensary of a chemist in the town. I walked there immediately and asked the lady behind the counter if I could speak to him. "George, somebody here wants a word with you."

George came out from the back room and stood behind the counter, surprised to see me. "Hello, Frances. What are ye doing here? Are ye not working today?"

"I've got something I need to tell ye. Can ye come here for a wee minute?" George stepped out from behind the counter and wandered off with me. The lady didn't look so happy at missing our conversation.

"What is it, Frances? What happened?" George looked a little worried.

"Doctor McMullan told me I had to tell ye, and I didn't want to tell ye when Paddy was around. I'm having a baby, and you're the father."

His jaw dropped, and he stared at me for a moment, letting the news sink in. Then, a spark of excitement ignited in his eyes. "That's fantastic! I'm going to be a dad," he exclaimed, his voice filled with joy. "I hope it's a boy; we can call him Bruce Lee. We'll have to see a priest and get married soon," he announced, already making plans for our future together. It felt that everything was moving too fast.

George had once expressed his desire to marry me to my sister, and now it appeared that his words were coming true. At that moment, a realisation dawned on me: perhaps this was why he had behaved the way he did that dreadful night. Everything had changed so swiftly; my future suddenly seemed predetermined. When I had risen that morning, I had never imagined I would be contemplating marriage, especially not to George. Despite my reservations about spending the rest of my life with him, I pushed those thoughts aside for the time being. This situation felt as though I had no other choice but to accept this new reality. It's what was expected of a pregnant girl at that time if she wanted to save her reputation.

Instead, I focused my thoughts on my unborn child. I was determined to be the best mother possible, providing all the love and attention that I had longed for but never received. The prospect of becoming a mother filled me with a sense of anticipation and joy. I couldn't wait to shower my baby with all the love and care he or she deserved.

"I'd better get back to work now, but I'll see ye later," George said, still beaming with pride.

At the McConnell's, everyone was eager to hear how my morning had gone. However, I wasn't ready to share the news about the baby just yet. Instead, I assured them that everything had gone smoothly and that I was feeling much better now. Mrs McConnell kindly insisted that I take the rest of the day off, allowing me some time to recuperate.

Retreating to my room, I lay on my bed, lost in thoughts of the future. As I imagined myself with a baby, I couldn't help but wonder what he or she would look like. Despite George's preference for a boy, I found myself envisioning a little girl adorned in frilly dresses with curls cascading down her back. The thought filled me with a sense of warmth and anticipation, and I eagerly awaited the day when I would hold her in my arms and shower her with all the love I had to give.

Although I now understood how I had become pregnant, the process of childbirth remained a mystery to me, and perhaps that was for the best. If I had known the details, I likely would have been overwhelmed with fear and anxiety. In my mind, there was no concept of the baby being born in the traditional sense: instead, I imagined that he or she would simply appear in my arms, a beautiful and miraculous gift, but somewhere, in the back of my mind, I knew the reason was that I didn't want to know. It would be time enough when it was happening.

All I could comprehend, at that moment, was that I had approximately seven more months until the baby would arrive. For now, I would cherish every moment of anticipation and excitement, eagerly awaiting the day when I would finally hold my child in my arms.

The following night, I found myself ready early, waiting anxiously on the road for Paddy and George. Pacing back and forth, I lit one cigarette after another, the familiar act offering a brief distraction from my swirling thoughts. No one had mentioned anything about not smoking when pregnant yet, it was the early seventies and back then it seemed like everyone smoked. Fortunately though, the cigarettes were starting to make me feel queasy, which was the last thing I needed on top of the morning sickness, so I had no choice but to stop.

I couldn't shake the nagging worry that George might have confided in Paddy about our situation. I desperately hoped he hadn't. I wasn't prepared to discuss marriage or where we would live. If he started pressing me on those topics, I knew I'd be heading straight back to the safety of the McConnell's home. Everything was moving too fast, and I felt overwhelmed and desperately needing time to adjust to this new reality. I didn't like my options. The thought of marrying George made me desperately unhappy, but I also knew I wouldn't want to be an unmarried mother. However, the one thing I was absolutely sure of was that I wanted my baby more than anything.

I grappled with conflicting emotions, torn between the unhappiness at the thought of marrying George and the fear of being an unmarried mother. Yet, amidst all the uncertainty, one thing remained clear: I wanted my baby more than anything in the world.

When they finally arrived, George greeted me with a beaming smile of pride, his excitement palpable. Paddy, ever curious, couldn't resist prodding George, wanting to know the source of his happiness. Determined to maintain a sense of normalcy, I joined in with Paddy's teasing, trying to divert attention away from George's jubilant mood. Despite Paddy's persistent questioning, George remained tight-lipped, his grin never faltering. Eventually, Paddy relented, realising he wouldn't get any answers from George.

We hung out as usual, but everything felt different. The weight of my secret hung heavy in the air. Despite our attempts to carry on as usual, the unspoken secret weighed heavily between us.

When George momentarily excused himself to greet an acquaintance, I seized the opportunity to confide in Paddy, pulling him aside to share the harrowing details of that fateful night. In hushed tones, I poured out my heart, laying bare the gravity of the predicament I now found myself in. I saw his jaw drop as he took in what I was saying.

"I knew something was going on, but I never imagined it was anything like this. I was worried that ye were drifting away from me. Ye haven't been yourself lately, but now it all makes sense," Paddy exclaimed, the shock evident in his voice. "Holy shit, Frances! What are ye going to do?"

His words echoed my inner turmoil, highlighting the gravity of the situation. The weight of uncertainty bore down on me as I grappled with the enormity of the decisions that lay ahead.

I was relieved that I'd put Paddy straight about a few things and asked him to explain my situation to his family. He told me I might have to go on the run again, but where could I go? Ye could hide out at my house: ye know ma would be happy to help ye."

I thought for a moment or two about what Paddy was suggesting. "But I would be trapped and couldn't leave the house, ever." It was a frightening thought. "We could try to make some kind of a plan, but how do we keep George out of the way?"

There was too much to think about and not much time, as George was already rushing ahead with arrangements for us to meet with the local Catholic priest.

Over the next weeks, George and I started spending time at his mum's house because, once we got married, I would be living with them. He was with them, and he wanted them to get to know me better.

Paddy couldn't understand why I let George talk me into it, as it was apparent to everyone that George's mother couldn't stand me. Without any family to support me, it didn't seem like I had any choice. She'd told Paddy that I wasn't good enough to hang around with her son and that he needed someone better. I assumed this was because I'd been raised in an orphanage. I tried to be nice to her, but it made no difference. Her mind was made up.

I was still feeling sick, several times daily, but I was coping and looking healthy enough to fool people for the moment. Until now, I hadn't felt like confiding in anyone at the McConnell house. However, this morning I'd awoken with an urge to unburden myself and decided to tell Susan. The morning passed slowly, and I became increasingly nervous.

When we finally stopped for a break, I blurted it out. "Susan, I'm going to have a wee baby."

She choked on a puff of her cigarette and looked at me in disbelief. "Frances, are yeah having me on? I shook my head, and she hugged me.

"Ye poor wee thing, what will ye do? I'll start knitting some baby clothes for ye." She was extremely good at knitting. We had a good talk until the break finished. It was great to finally talk to someone in the house and get it off my chest.

As the days passed, the weight of my secret weighed heavier on my mind. I knew that I couldn't keep it hidden much longer, but the fear of losing my job was paralysing.

We talked about it again at lunchtime and at every break after that. Over the next few days, Susan ever the voice of reason, urged me to confide in Mrs McConnell, convinced that she would understand and offer her support, especially considering my plans to marry.

I wanted to mention it but couldn't get the words out. I wasn't sure how she would take it: the McConnell's were a devout Catholic family, deeply rooted in their faith and guided by strict Catholic values. Also, I was apprehensive about losing my job; I needed the money to save up for baby things and had nowhere else to go.

Despite my apprehensions, I knew that I couldn't delay the inevitable forever. But for now, I decided to bide my time, waiting until I had a clearer plan. And as the days stretched on, I clung to the hope that I would find a way forward, a path that would lead me to a brighter future for myself and my unborn child.

The revelation of my pregnancy seemed to strip away any of my choices, as everyone around me began dictating what they believed to be the best course of action. Despite the initial shock, the McConnell's accepted the situation, assuming that marriage was the inevitable next step for the sake of the baby's well-being. It felt as though I was being swept along by the expectations and assumptions of others, with little room for my own desires or preferences.

Continuing to work at the McConnell's became increasingly challenging as my pregnancy progressed, ultimately reaching a point where I felt compelled to resign. Departing on amicable terms, I was reassured by their genuine desire to stay in touch and to help where they could and I promised to keep them updated on my well-being and that of the baby.

Mr McConnell's words about life and choices echoed in my mind. As I pondered the events that led me to this point, a sense of resignation and fatalism washed over me. It was as if fate, the influence of others, and perhaps even a higher power had conspired to shape the trajectory of my life, leaving me feeling like a mere pawn in a larger game.

In a world where decisions were seemingly made for me rather than by me, I couldn't help but question if anyone truly cared about my feelings or desires. The weight of others' expectations pressed down upon me, leaving little room for my own autonomy or aspirations. It was a stark realisation, and I longed for a sense of control over my own destiny.

The Wedding

It was my wedding day, and I woke at five twenty feeling sick. I felt that strong impulse to run, to pack up my few belongings and get as far away from Omagh as possible, but I had a baby to consider. Anyway, where would I run to? I was trapped. It felt strange having to consider my baby; nothing else in this world would have stopped me from running.

The modest four-bedroom house would now contain eight people. With my arrival, the household had swelled to include George and myself, George's parents, his youngest sister, an older brother, and two younger brothers who were forced to share a room.

As if the crowded quarters weren't already strained enough, the older brother's new girlfriend was expected to move in soon, further exacerbating the situation. Fortunately, two older brothers and an older sister had already flown the nest, having married and established their own households.

Our room was a small box room, barely large enough to accommodate a single bed. Neglected and in need of refurbishment for years, the heavily flowered wallpaper was badly faded and coming unstuck at the edges. The old yellow and brown striped curtains, framing the window didn't fit in with anything else, adding to the room's dishevelled appearance. The furniture, too, was neglected and a haphazard assembly. Each piece seemed to serve a functional purpose only.

As I surveyed its dilapidated confines, I couldn't help but feel a pang of resignation, a recognition that this cramped space reflected the limitations and constraints that governed my existence. I would miss my home at the McConnell's.

After the wedding, I would be sharing this with George. That thought sent a shiver through me. I tried to push it from my mind because I didn't know how I was going to cope. I'd felt miserably sad on the day I moved out of the McConnell's and into George's home. It was apparent that Mrs McAteer, George's mother, didn't want me there and didn't want her son to marry me. She had voiced her opinions loudly enough for the whole housing estate to hear, insisting she would not attend the wedding. She even suggested that I'd gotten myself pregnant just to trap George. Growing up in an orphanage had caused me to be unsuitable. I could never be good enough to marry into her family.

I'd crept down to the kitchen before anyone had woken. The sound of the kettle boiling seemed louder in the silent house, and I was worried it would wake anyone who was a light sleeper. When my tea was made, I looked about to see where I could sit, but no sooner had I sat than I was back up on my feet again: I felt caged, like an animal, pacing back and forth in the small kitchen. Once again, the urge to get out and run was strong. I felt tears running down my face, dripping onto my dressing gown.

As I sipped the tea, thoughts of Sinead filled my mind. I wanted her close to me now. She was my only family, and I wanted her with me for my wedding. I had tried to contact her about the wedding but had been told she'd left the convent and was living somewhere in Belfast. She had moved from her original accommodation, and the nuns were still trying to find out where she was. I knew she would have come, if she could, but I would have to deal with it alone.

I tried to imagine how she would have reacted to my predicament. She had never liked George, and I knew she'd have tried desperately to talk me out of it. Perhaps, between us, we could have found a solution. How could I be back in this situation again: alone and frightened?

Suddenly, I felt nauseous and dashed to the bathroom, making it just in time before throwing up again. I hated feeling like this, but I'd gotten used to the idea that this was how it would be until the baby was born. At least there would be a baby at the end of it. I was hugely excited about that and tried to convince myself that the baby would make everything worthwhile. It was almost six-thirty, and I returned to my bedroom before anyone else stirred.

Later, sitting on the bed, I could hear Mrs McAteer talking to George outside the door. "It's not too late to change your mind, George. Sure, you probably aren't even the father anyway."

George mumbled something back, which I couldn't make out, and then they went downstairs.

I dreaded having to come out of the room and face her. She would say something to make me feel worthless. I knew today she would be even worse. I sat in the bedroom, unable to move, regretting I hadn't run earlier when I had the chance. As I considered what life had in store for me now, floods of tears ran down my face. I tried hard to pull myself together, telling myself that having survived the convent,

I could survive anything, including this marriage. I dried the tears, took a deep breath and braced myself for the inevitable.

Most of the family were up now; I could hear them talking in the living room. As I opened the door, the smell of bacon wafted from the kitchen. Usually, I would have loved that smell, but now it turned my stomach, so I had no choice but to dash downstairs to the bathroom. The door was locked. I banged on it urgently and George shouted, "I'll be out in a wee minute."

Standing in the hall, listening to Mrs McAteer run me down, I felt overwhelmed. I'd noticed that she had started referring to me as "Reilly" with that same tone the nuns had used. "Max, ye should be talking your son out of this ridiculous marriage to that Reilly bitch," she scolded. "Would I be the only one who can see what she's after?" she continued,

"Don't be so ridiculous now. George knows what he's doing; if he doesn't, he'll have to learn from his mistakes. Sure, it's not as if we've got money or anything else she'd want. She'd have picked on someone else if she'd wanted that, now, wouldn't she?" he argued, trying to be rational and calm things down.

Max was a lovely man with a good heart. I had never heard him speak badly of anyone. He would often stick up for me when his awful wife was bullying me. Unfortunately, when he wasn't working, he usually went to the pub or maybe went fishing anywhere to escape his nagging wife. I couldn't imagine why they were together as there seemed to be nothing but animosity between them.

George came out of the bathroom, and I dashed past him, locked the door and started throwing up again.

Max knew that I'd heard everything. I listened to him tell his wife to be quiet, explaining that I had been outside the door. I was still bent over the toilet when the arguing flared up again. I covered my ears with my hands, trying to block it out.

"I don't care if that wee bitch hears me," she yelled back at him.

"It'll soon be too late, George, if we can't talk ye out of marrying that wee bitch now. Ye can do a lot better than her."

"I'm getting married today, Ma, and she's having my kid; there's nothing anyone can do about it now," George shouted back at her.

Soon, they were all shouting, and my head was spinning. As soon as I felt well enough, I returned to the bedroom, shut myself in and stayed until the arguing stopped.

A short while later, George asked if I was all right. I didn't feel like talking to him, so I nodded that I was.

"Don't take any notice of me, Ma. I think she's been at the drink all night. We'll be grand, ye know, just wait and see. We'll get our names down for a council house, and everything will improve. I promise, ye,"

I didn't answer; I was afraid of what might come out of my mouth. By now, I was an expert at bottling up my feelings. I'd been doing it since I was a small child.

"Well, you'll have to get yourself ready to go to the chapel now, Frances. I can't find anyone to give us a lift. We'll walk into town and get there in plenty of time."

After all the arguing, his voice sounded calm, but he still looked annoyed.

"Right then, I'll be getting ready now," I said, fumbling about with the clothes. I'd sorted out a pair of black trousers, boots, a red jumper and a midi-length coat with fake fur around the hood the night before.

We were to be married at the big Sacred Heart chapel in town. Only four of us would be at the service: myself, George, George's brother, John, and his new girlfriend. John was to be George's best man, and his girlfriend, whom I'd not yet met, would be my bridesmaid. Afterwards, the four of us would drink at the Royal Arms Hotel. George was looking forward to this most of all. It was his wedding day, and he'd planned to get very drunk.

I knew him well enough by now to know that he didn't want to use any of our money for a taxi because there'd be less for a drink, so we were walking. It certainly wasn't the wedding I had dreamed of having someday. As we left the house, no one was around to wave us off or wish us luck. I didn't care at that point, although George seemed to. I was just pleased that we'd escaped without another shouting match. We began the walk into town, which would take us about half an hour.

I was soon shivering as the icy wind cut into my face. Neither of us spoke until we reached the chapel and met the priest. We shook hands and then he took us to the sacristy and asked us to sit. He then proceeded to lecture us on the sacrament of matrimony. I wasn't listening, just going through the motions. It seemed ironic that he should be preaching to us about good virtues as it was only eleven thirty in the morning and he already smelled heavily of whiskey.

I started to panic, realising that I would become George's wife in a matter of minutes. It was my worst nightmare. I knew this was my last chance to run. If I wanted to leave this marriage, I must go now. I was in panic mode, thinking I had left it too late, but had I? The lengthy lecture finished, and we walked back into the chapel.

"Ye can wait here a while until your best man turns up. I'll be off and get myself ready for this union," the priest mumbled while walking back to the sacristy.

I needed an excuse to leave the chapel and run away from George. I kept telling myself, 'Do it, Frances, go now, run for your life.' I was going to do it; I was going to get away. The panic in me was getting worse. "I'll be back in a wee minute, George. I've just got to go to the toilet. You wait here for John and Flossy," I said, trembling.

"Where are you going to find a toilet?"

"I'll go across to the Golden Griddle. They'll let me use their's," I said. Desperate to get away; I stepped out into the fresh air, hoping never to see George again. I noticed he'd followed me, watching where I was going while he lit a cigarette.

"I'll wait for ye here then. Don't be long, or we'll be keeping the priest waiting," he shouted after me, keeping a close watch on me as I crossed the road.

My heart raced, and I could hear it beating loudly and clearly. I would run for it as soon as I was out of sight. The realisation that I couldn't marry George was now fixed in my mind. I couldn't return to Mrs McAteer's house. There was no turning back now that I'd decided; I had to stick with it. I'd thumb down the first car I saw and wouldn't even care where it was going. The adrenaline started to flow, and that familiar mixture of excitement and fear hit me. George was out of sight now, so I began to run, heading out of town. Just a few more minutes, and I'll be free.!

"Frances, stop. Where are ye going?" someone shouted. I looked back and saw George's cousin running after me. I didn't know what to say and tried to get my head straight.

"George is waiting for ye outside the chapel. I was just talking to him. He said if I see ye, to say the priest is waiting. John and his woman are already there."

This was the last thing I needed: How could I get rid of him? "I'm just trying to find a toilet. I'll be fine, James. I'll get there soon enough," I explained, but I couldn't even convince myself. I should have just carried on running!

"Well, ye won't be finding one out here. Try one of the shops or cafes in the town," James suggested while giving me the strangest look.

"Yeah, I was going to try the Golden Griddle, but it looked packed," I lied, hoping he wouldn't notice.

"Come on, Frances, I'll walk back with ye, and we will explain to them that you're getting married in a few minutes. They'll let ye go on in." Grabbing my arm, he rushed me back towards the cafe. It was almost empty when we arrived.

"It's not packed now, Frances, look! Ye must have imagined it," he said, trying to take the mickey out of me.

"I think I have wedding jitters. Please leave me alone." By the time I got back, George was pacing back and forth angrily outside the chapel.

"You took your bloody time," he said angrily. Fortunately, I didn't have to explain as the priest came out and said he was ready for us.

The large chapel felt bleak, cold, empty and oppressive with just the five of us inside. As we walked down the long aisle, I found it impossible to keep my emotions in check and by the time we reached the altar, I was sobbing like a baby. I felt defeated and utterly miserable on what should have been the happiest day of my life.

The priest was concerned and went to the sacristy, returning a few moments later with a box of tissues. He offered them to me and asked if I was sure that I wanted him to continue. George told him that I did, and it was my hormones that were all over the place with the pregnancy. I was just overexcited, he explained to the confused priest. Unfortunately, he seemed to accept the explanation and proceeded.

The service seemed to go on for ages, as did the tears; there was no way out now. When George slipped the small gold ring on my finger, I sensed an instant change in his attitude. He smirked, like he had sealed some big deal, and seemed full of self-importance and arrogance. I felt frightened, seeing him look at me like I was his possession.

The service finished, and the priest made the sign of the cross. "Peace be with ye both," he said.

We left the chapel, and the cold air made me shiver. My teeth chattered uncontrollably. Then, to my surprise, Susan appeared before us, throwing confetti everywhere. My coat was covered in it. She jumped up and down, shouting her congratulations at us. I missed her, and it was terrific to see her again. She had brought her camera to take a few pictures of us. We posed for her, and I forced myself to look happy.

"I've got to get back to work now, Frances, but I'll see ye soon," she said and hugged me.

"Thanks for coming, Susan,"

George told me to hold his arm while we walked to the hotel. "My hands are freezing, George. I need to keep them in my pockets," I said, shivering.

"You're my wife now, and you'll bloody do as I say," he snapped at me. John and Flossy looked shocked but said nothing. There was a tone in his voice that I'd not heard before, and I sensed that this wasn't a good time to argue with him, so I did as he ordered. However, I was angry about how he spoke to me but even angrier with James for bringing me back. Still, it was hard to believe that someone could change so quickly. Perhaps this was what he had been waiting for all along, and he'd been holding back, worried that I might leave him.

George stared at me, and I felt different. Not at all myself. He made me feel like I was no longer a person, just an extension of him with no mind of my own.

The bar in the Royal Arms Hotel was warm and comfortable, and we settled ourselves at one of the tables with our drinks. George made it very clear to me that no wife of his was going to be drinking and told me I was having orange juice. It was a decision that had nothing to do with me being pregnant. It sounded very much like this was how things were going to be from now on. He believed that Irish men had the right to drink while their women's place was in the home: cleaning and looking after their husband and the children. We had only been married a few minutes, and already it was becoming clear how things would be. He was setting down the orders that he wanted me to obey.

George and John drank their first few pints as though they feared the pub would run out of beer. Then they were on to pints and whiskey chasers. George soon let everyone know that he'd just married and thoroughly enjoyed the free drinks which came his way, ordering one for me and drinking it himself. By early afternoon, the bar was packed, and people were shouting to make themselves heard. My head was beginning to spin, but I tried to look as though I was enjoying myself. John didn't hang around for long. His mother wouldn't have wanted him to.

People were coming over to congratulate us, mostly men, many of whom knew George. The family were well-known in the town. George's oldest brother, Frank, was an Elvis look-alike, and he mimicked his songs so well that people said he sounded exactly like Elvis. His concerts were popular and made him famous locally. George loved that people knew he was Frank's brother. He enjoyed living under Frank's shadow as he felt he didn't need to achieve anything for himself - except to be like Bruce Lee.

The men in the bar offered advice on how to make our marriage last. They were all experts, or so it seemed. The most important secret to a good marriage was not to nag at your husband, especially when he has been out drinking all day in the pub.

"A man had a God-given right to drink," they insisted, and George agreed and staggered up to the bar for another pint. This was going to be my life, I thought.

Apart from the staff, I was now the only sober person in the bar. I watched as the people around me became increasingly drunk, and their conversations became increasingly difficult to understand.

George returned from the bar with a few more men he'd persuaded to buy him more drinks. He started singing Elvis songs, and others soon joined in. I felt embarrassed at how awful it sounded. He didn't have his brother's talent, and it didn't help that he was drunk. George was soon singing at the top of his voice, and it was clear that he thought he sounded great. The drinking and singing carried on for the rest of the afternoon.

Later that evening, George's brother, Frank, turned up with a friend. Everyone was making a fuss about him like he was a pop star. Eventually, he managed to get away and came over to sit with us. He seemed surprised to see us. I had met him only a few times before, although I'd heard his family talk about him often. He was their golden boy and had done them proud. Frank looked and sounded like a clone of Elvis. He put a great deal of work into his voice, which was great, and he had the walk, hairstyle, and sideboards down to a tee. I found it hard not to stare at him.

"Congratulations, George," he said, patting him on the back. Then he leaned towards me, put his arm around me and kissed me on the cheek.

Congratulations, Ma said ye would be here. Let me get ye newlyweds a drink," he said, calling one of the staff over to the table. He ordered cheap champagne and some glasses. Frank poured and toasted George and me, saying he hoped we would be delighted to be married. I lifted my glass to take a small sip, but George gave me a look, so I put it back on the table. He didn't have to say a word. He didn't want me to drink, and I didn't want to make a scene.

After the champagne, Frank said he was going up the road to his mother's and asked if we wanted a lift. George accepted and said it would probably break the ice with his mother if we went in with Frank. As much as I hated being with George, I didn't want to return to the house, but I knew I would have too eventually.

We left the bar with George staggering all over the place. Frank laughed at the sight of him and warned him that he'd have a bad head in the morning. When we pulled up outside the house, the lights were on and we could see that most of the family was in. We followed Frank through the front door and into the living room. I wasn't expecting a warm welcome, but I had hoped I would be ignored now that Frank was there. Perhaps I could sneak to the bedroom and leave them with Mrs McAteer.

Everyone was sitting around a roaring fire, and the heat hit me as soon as I entered the room. Frank went over to where his mother sat drinking and kissed her. There was an empty gin bottle on the table beside her, and she looked like she'd been drinking all day. The atmosphere in the room was tense. George's brothers and sister looked uncomfortable and wouldn't look at us. No one spoke, but I felt sure they'd been talking about us before we arrived.

"How are ye, Ma," Frank asked, breaking the awkward silence.

"How do ye fucking think I am, Frank," she hollered at the top of her voice. "Your brother has gone and married that fucking charity case. He could have done better for himself, but he wouldn't fucking listen, would he? Oh no, he had to fucking go and do it, didn't he," she exploded.

"Come on, Ma, don't upset yourself like this," Frank insisted, trying to calm her.

Shaking with anger and embarrassment and unable to stop crying, I turned to walk out of the door. Just then, Mrs McAteer got up from her chair and hurled her glass across the room at me, shouting.

"Yeah fucking bitch.!" The glass smashed against the door above my head, and shards of glass fell onto my head and face. "This sham of a marriage won't last if I've got anything to do with it," she yelled. "The nuns should have kept you locked up in that convent and never have fucking let you out!"

George told his mother to sit down and shut up. But soon, everyone was shouting and screaming, making it almost impossible to determine what was being said. I ran to the bathroom, sobbing, somehow I needed to clean myself up and try to calm down.

How on earth was I going to survive living in this house? Mrs McAteer hated me, and there was nothing I could do about that. However, she had said she would ensure the marriage wouldn't last. That would be doing me a favour because I didn't want it to last, either.

I knew the rest of the family didn't mind George marrying me, and when their mother wasn't around, they spoke to me normally. However, she was a bitter and twisted woman who wanted to control everyone's life. If you went against her wishes, you were in trouble. She didn't seem to care how bad she made people feel, especially when it was me.

Additionally, she loved to pile on the guilt, trying to make the family feel indebted to her. She'd go on and on about the terrible labour pains she'd suffered and how her children owed her something for going through it. Then, she would remind them of what an excellent job she'd done of bringing them all up and how she always put them first. The guilt trip usually worked, but she'd create a scene when it didn't, just like she was doing now. I couldn't understand why they let her get away with it.

Despite the noise from the living room, I could hear the front door knocker banging. Frank called my name and said it was someone for me. I couldn't think who it could be, but I wiped my eyes and went to the door. The sight of Sinead made me burst into tears again, and I rushed to hug her.

"Thank God you're here Sinead, I've been trying to find ye. I can't ask ye in, but I'll come out," I sobbed.

She looked concerned, "What the hell's been going on, Frances? Are ye all right?"

I didn't dare answer because I didn't want George's family to hear me. Holding on to her arm, I guided her to a bench across the road where we could get some privacy. We sat there shivering and talked. She told me she'd gone to the McConnell's house to see me, and they told her I was living up here with George's family.

"Come on, Frances. Just tell me what's going on," she insisted. I was still sobbing uncontrollably at the mess I was in. I managed to blurt everything out to her. She sat there, momentarily stunned, trying to let it all sink in. She turned to me and said, "Ye got married today, and you're going to have a baby?" she said, obviously wanting me to confirm that she'd heard me right. I nodded and told her I'd tried to find her and tell her what was happening. I explained that the nuns said they didn't know her address. She was fuming at what George and his family had done to me, but she was also very sad for me.

"What are ye going to do, Frances? Ye can't stay here: ye know it will drive ye mental! Come back with me, and we will find somewhere for ye to hide."

"I don't have any choice. What else can I do, Sinead? I'm pregnant, and I've nowhere else to go." We sat shivering while thinking about the situation for a few minutes.

Sinead jumped up and started shouting in the direction of George's house, "Ye fucking bastard, George, look what ye did to my sister. I hate the fucking lot of ye. If ye touch my sister again, I'll fucking kill ye."

Sinead had an awful temper, and it often got her in trouble. But I couldn't remember her standing up for me so passionately before. Although I appreciated it now, I didn't want her to get into trouble with the McAteer's. She was angry enough to take them on, but I didn't want her to get hurt. I was so protective of Sinead that I would have joined in, which would have made my situation a lot more complicated.

"Sinead, you'll only make things worse for me!" I pleaded. "I will have to go back and face them." Reluctantly, she came and sat back down beside me.

"Come to Belfast with me then, Frances. I've got a lift back tonight, Ye can't go back in there." she insisted.

"What would I do in Belfast Sinead, and where the fuck would I live?"

"I don't know, but I can't take you to where I'm staying. We could ask around and find someone's couch until we can find you a place. It wouldn't be a problem, and I'm sure it will work out fine," she insisted.

Things would have been so different if I'd got away that morning and made a run for it at the church. I would have taken my chances and not come back. However, now that I was married, it seemed to me that George owned me and would get the police to track me down, just like the nuns had done when I was in the convent. Normally, I would have let my sister talk me into anything, even if I knew it wouldn't work out. I now felt different about everything and feared what might happen to me. I was someone's property, and I was pregnant. I wouldn't say I liked it, but that's how it was, and I felt powerless about it.

"Frances. I'm sure we'll find ye somewhere to stay!"

"But I could get stuck, Sinead; I'd be walking around Belfast, pregnant. On the run and this bloody awful weather isn't going to help. I need to have somewhere to go. With no money and no friends, I could end up homeless, and they might even take the baby away from me. I must stay here: no one else will have me! I don't have a choice, so please don't go on about it. It's hard enough!" I sobbed.

Sinead thought I was mad to stay but she eventually gave up asking me to leave. She had blind faith that someplace would magically turn up when we got to Belfast. Sinead believed I could live happily away from George, but I had to live in the real world.

Changing the subject, I asked her about her job at an old people's home in Belfast. She told me about an older woman who always pretended to be dead. She was so good at it that sometimes the staff and doctors weren't sure if she was dead. She could slow her heart rate down, making it hard to get a pulse. Then, when everyone was sure she was dead, she would get up and start walking around. Sinead was laughing about it.

She went on, "Anyway, the other morning, I got to work, and Rosy was sitting in her chair, looking as dead as a doornail. I'd been told to get her to eat her porridge. Come on now, Rosy, eat this up for me, I said. Then I shoved a spoonful into her mouth, and she just sat there rigidly. Then, it all ran out of her mouth and down her chin. I told her to stop messing about. I kept feeding her for ages until I got fed up with it. By then, she was in a right mess."

"I was so annoyed with her for playing games and told her we wouldn't be getting the doctor again. I explained we had sick people here who we could be attending to. Then, I stormed off and told my boss, and she said that I should just ignore her. So, I did; I ignored her for most of the day. Finally, when I returned to her room, she was still sitting in the same position. My boss got the doctor, and he told us that she had died this time, sometime during the night,"

We sat on the bench, laughing at Sinead's story. I wasn't sure that caring for the elderly was the best job for Sinead. She didn't have the patience or compassion required for the job.

"I felt awful, Frances, for shoving the porridge into her while she was dead. How the hell was I supposed to know? Anyway, that's what she gets for all her practical jokes."

"How did you know that she was dead this time?" I asked.

"She'd fucking better be! She's buried now," Sinead laughed so much, and I enjoyed listening to her. I couldn't remember when I'd last had a good laugh. Everything had been so stressful recently, and there wasn't much to laugh about. I had stopped noticing how cold it was and enjoyed listening to a few more of her work stories.

Eventually, a car pulled up, and Sinead said it was her lift. As I got up to hug her, I noticed George propped up against the front door of his house. He had been spying on us. Sinead handed me a piece of paper with her address on it. "Look after yourself, Frances. Sure, I'll be back soon enough to see ye. Write and let me know all the gossip." We hugged, and she wandered over to the car. Meanwhile, George was staggering over towards me.

"Frances, get yourself indoors before ye get pneumonia," he slurred.

We returned to the house with George leaning on me for support. The house was quiet now, and we went straight up to the small bedroom where I had woken up earlier that morning. George threw himself onto the bed and began snoring within seconds. He looked completely out of it, and I breathed a sigh of relief. At least now, I wouldn't have to worry about what my wedding night might bring.

There wasn't any room left in the bed, but that didn't worry me because it spared me from having to get in next to him. Instead, I sat on the carpet with a cigarette in hand and an ashtray by my side. I rested my head against the wall. It was the first moment of peace I'd had all day. What a mess!

For the first time in my life everything had been going well. I should have realised it wouldn't last.

Bloody Sunday

"What the hell are ye doing on the floor?" George shouted at me as he staggered towards the bedroom door the next morning.

"Well, ye fell asleep on the bed, George. There wasn't any room, so I lay down here," I explained. He looked at me strangely, then disappeared downstairs, grunting and moaning.

I yawned and stretched out, trying to rid myself of the cold stiffness in my body, then scrambled up onto the warm comfort of the bed. I hadn't slept much during the night, just managing the occasional doze with my head against the wall. It hadn't been much of a way to spend my wedding night, but it was still much better than the alternative. I thought that was probably not what Doctor McMullan had in mind when he'd pleaded with me to take good care of myself.

I lay there quietly, listening to George fumbling about in the bathroom. Other family members were up now, and I could make out Mrs McAteer's voice and two of George's brothers. At some stage, I would have to go down and face all of them, but right now, just the thought of facing her made me feel sick. I pulled the covers over my shoulders and tried to imagine I was back at the McConnell's home - safe and happy. Without meaning to, I drifted off into a deep sleep.

Sometime later, the sound of raised voices woke me. "Here's your breakfast, George. Ye know that wee bitch upstairs should be making it for ye now," she yelled. "Does she think this is a bloody hotel or something?"

"Now that you've married her, you'll have to sort her out, George, and let her know what's what."

"Leave the wee girl alone now: I'm sure she's exhausted. She'll not want to see any of this family now, not after the episode ye caused yesterday," Max said in my defence.

"That's typical of you, Max," she yelled at him. "Ye take everyone else's side but your wife's."

I couldn't handle hearing any more arguing, so I blocked my ears with my fingers and buried my head under the pillow. I felt grateful to Max for trying to defend me, and I admired his courage in standing up to her like that. I'm sure it couldn't have been easy for him, being married to her.

A few minutes later, when I removed my fingers from my ears, I noticed the arguing had stopped. I curled myself up in a ball and drifted back to sleep, wishing I didn't have to wake up again.

"Are ye staying in bed all day then?" George asked in a sarcastic tone as he shook my shoulder.

"I can't go down there: your mother hates me," I answered while bursting into tears.

"Ye'll have to come down eventually, Frances. Come on down with me now and stop crying like that. If me Ma sees ye, it'll only get worse."

"I can't go down, George. I'd rather just stay up here," I pleaded, but George was having none of it. There was no point in arguing with him, so I got to my feet, wiped away the tears, and dressed.

Everyone turned and stared as we entered the living room, but no one spoke. The atmosphere was tense, and I wasn't sure how to respond. I felt humiliated when George ordered me to put the kettle on.

"That will be six mugs," he shouted as I entered the kitchen.

So, this is how it's going to be, I thought. George acting out like he's on some big ego trip. Bossing me around to prove to his mother what a big man he was. Right there and then, it felt like I was back in the convent, except here it was Mrs McAteer instead of the nuns.

When I returned with the tea. Mrs McAteer's eyes bore into me, and she was looking for any excuse to criticise me. Avoiding eye contact, I placed the mugs carefully on the coffee table.

I was retreating to the safety of the bathroom when she shouted, "Reilly! You've forgotten the biscuits. They're on the top shelf of the cupboard."

I cringed, why was it that people like her and the nuns couldn't address me by my Christian name? I was sure she knew how much it upset me. Why couldn't they just ask instead of ordering me about like a slave? I wanted to scream back at her, but I had been conditioned not to answer.

"I'll be going to town soon," Mrs McAteer informed me. "So, when I've gone, ye can clean the house to earn your keep."

Alone in the bathroom, I seriously contemplated taking my own life. Then, the thought of the child I was carrying flooded my mind, and

I knew I couldn't subject my unborn baby to such a fate. I yearned to be a mother and was determined to break the cycle of dysfunction passed down by my mother, the nuns and Mrs McAteer. My child would feel loved and cherished, unlike the upbringing I had.

So, despite the overwhelming despair, I resolved to find a way to cope. Perhaps Sinead was right, and I should have returned to Belfast with her. Maybe I should have placed my trust in 'the universe' to protect me. However, my cynicism ran deep, and I found it hard to believe that good things could happen to me. After all, I had experienced horrific traumas as a child, when I should have been shielded from harm. Why would it be any different now?

I hated how Mrs McAteer spoke to me and degraded me in front of everyone, and I knew I couldn't take much more of it, so I stayed locked in the bathroom until she left for the shops in town.

When I eventually heard the front door slam, I waited a few minutes longer to be sure she had gone. The house was quiet, and I appeared to be alone. I crept out and scanned each room, then checked the back garden, just in case. A few minutes later, I was sitting by the roaring fire with a cup of hot tea, I breathed a huge sigh of relief and relaxed into the armchair. It felt great to be on my own! I didn't care about having to do the housework just so long as Mrs McAteer wasn't around to torment me. For the first time in days, I felt at ease and relaxed in the chair.

Then, despite feeling sick, I forced myself to eat some toast. I wanted the baby to be healthy. Next, I looked through the record collection to find something cheerful to work to. There were many Elvis records, but I'd heard enough of him at my wedding. I got one of my own from the bedroom. My favourite singer at that time, Dave Edmonds, would be perfect. All day long, I washed, scrubbed, polished, hoovered and mopped. I worked to the sound of that same record until, finally, there was nothing more left for me to do; the house was spotless.

As none of the family had returned yet, I took advantage of the peace and ran myself a hot bath. It was the most relaxed I'd been in weeks. The water was hot and bubbly, and I was soon drifting off to sleep. When I awoke, the water had become lukewarm, and my skin was wrinkled. I felt refreshed and completely relaxed as I dressed and lay on my bed, waiting until someone came home.

Sometime later, I awoke to the sound of men's voices downstairs. I rubbed my eyes. How long had I been asleep? From the top of the stairs, I could hear Max and George's older brother, John, discussing something that had happened.

"Oh my God, it's downright disgraceful. When you think they're supposed to be protecting us over here!" Max sounded upset about something, so I listened for a while to fathom what was going on. "We should know more about it when the evening news comes on. Ye know that could happen to us soon, here in Omagh."

"It's bloody awful, Da. No one's safe!" John was distraught and angry about whatever they'd been watching.

"That's a fact, son, even when you're peacefully standing up for what's right."

I wondered what they were talking about. It sounded serious, and as I couldn't hear Mrs McAteer's voice, I wandered down to find out.

Max smiled and praised me for doing a grand job on the house. I thought it was nice of him to notice, especially given how distracted and sad he looked.

"What's happened, Max?" I asked, hoping not to sound too nosy. He invited me to sit with him, then explained that they'd just heard that the Army had fired shots into a crowd of peaceful protesters in Derry: men, women and children who had been protesting internment - the imprisonment without trial of young Catholic men - and against the brutality within the Maze prison and on board the prison ship HMS Maidstone.

Max explained that many Catholics had welcomed the troops when they first arrived. Some people even took cups of tea, sandwiches or scones out to the soldiers. They thought that they were there to keep the peace. However, as the violence increased, that relationship deteriorated, and since the introduction of internment, any remaining goodwill had disappeared. After this atrocity, he felt sure all Catholics would be against the army.

I knew some of what he was telling me from the news reports on television. Since the start of the internment, there have been reports of trouble almost every day. Recently, the Catholics had gone on a rent strike, refusing to pay their council rent or rates until internment ended.

When several internees escaped the prison ship a few weeks ago, everyone on the Catholic estates cheered for them. I remember feeling delighted even though I had no idea about the politics behind the Troubles. In the convent, we learned that Catholics had the one true faith, and the mere mention of the word Protestant was sufficient to warrant a look of disgust from the nuns. The Catholic nuns hated them with a passion, but there had never been any mention of the Troubles.

As he went on explaining things, Max couldn't help but share his anger toward the soldiers. As I listened, I felt sorrow for the families of those killed in Derry. Thinking about the life growing inside me, I tried to imagine the terrible pain and sense of loss that the families must be feeling.

Suddenly, there was a loud commotion as George and his youngest brother, Ed, bounded through the front door.

"Did ye hear the news, Daddy?" Ed blurted out, breathless, having run home to tell his dad.

"Yeah, I've heard, son." Max slumped forward, his head resting heavily in his hands. It was the first time I'd seen him so sad.

"Derry is only forty miles," said George, excitedly. "Next time, it could be us who'll be getting shot at."

Max tried to change the subject, telling George what a grand job I'd done on the house. George showed no interest and carried on talking about Derry.

I was still listening to them talk when Mrs McAteer returned. "Put the kettle on now, Reilly, and make everyone some tea!" she ordered.

"Leave the wee girl alone now, will ye!" Max moaned. "Would ye look at how clean the place is? She's been cleaning all fucking day. Someone should be making her a cup of tea. I've never seen this place looking so clean. Give the girl a break, would ye?"

Mrs McAteer was fuming. "It won't do her any harm," she insisted spitefully. "And it will help pay her way while living under this roof." I could see that Max was annoyed as I headed out of the room. From the kitchen, I could still hear them arguing. Max told her that, as George and I were married and I was having his baby, I should be treated more like one of the family. He even suggested that George should take more responsibility for caring for me. I was pleased with his support, but Mrs McAteer would have none of it and accused me of being a scheming little slut!

"Ye see, Reilly, look what you've fucking caused now!" she screeched at the top of her voice, and fury in her eyes. She hated that Max was looking out for me. I burst into tears and ran upstairs. Max told her to calm down and stop picking on me. He was the only one who dared speak back to her that way, taking my side. I was grateful but knew it would make no difference.

Later, when the argument calmed down, Max knocked on the bedroom door and popped his head in. "I just want to see if you're okay, Frances. Now, don't ye take all that nonsense with my wife to heart.

You're doing just fine, and I'm sure you'll make a grand wee wife and mother."

His words were comforting, and I felt better knowing that somebody in the house understood what I was going through. I dried my eyes and tried to pull myself together. The door had been left open when he left to go downstairs, and I could now hear the television.

Sitting at the top of the stairs, I could hear the newsreader talking about Derry. He sounded sombre as he reported that thirteen men had been shot dead and at least thirteen others, including one woman, were injured. Gasps of horror came from downstairs.

I felt frightened, especially for my unborn child. It was not the best time to bring a baby into the world. I crept back downstairs to listen to what was being said and understand how bad things could get. Fortunately, no one even noticed me sneak back into the living room.

"It's going to be a bloodbath now."

"Nothing can ever be right, not after what's happened today."

"There'll be even more violence now, all over Ulster."

It sounded so depressing, and it seemed impossible not to believe that the Troubles would worsen. There was a loud knock at the door, neighbours coming to see if we'd heard the news. Before long, everyone was outside, on the pavement, talking. Some of the women made the sign of the cross as they spoke of the dead. Someone suggested that the schools would be closed the following day as a mark of respect. It felt as though a dark cloud was hanging over all of us. I wished that somehow, I might get away from it all before my baby was born.

I went up to bed early that night, leaving George and his family to their conversations. Although I sympathised with everyone concerned, I couldn't bear to listen to any more speculation. Worrying thoughts of what might happen had everyone on edge. It played around in my head for a while but, eventually, I drifted off to sleep.

Sometime later, I woke up startled to find George had joined me and was penetrating me before I'd even woken! He would say it was his right now as I was his wife, his property. Luckily for me, it was always quick. He soon rolled over and fell asleep, leaving me feeling worthless and degraded.

Revelations

Over the next four months, life at George's grew even more challenging for me. Mrs McAteer continued to find any reason to harass me. I tried to stay out of her way as much as possible, which was awkward and usually meant hiding in my bedroom or the bathroom. Also, George's attitude towards me had worsened, especially when he'd been out drinking, which was all too often. When drunk, he would lash out at me, slapping me around the face and head. The following day, he'd always blame it on the drink. Whenever I threatened to leave him, he would promise to change. However, it would never last more than a few days.

Unfortunately, when he was at home, there was nowhere that I could hide. I felt trapped, and there was no one I could turn to for help. When I found myself on my own and at peace, I would lay on the bed with my hands on my stomach, feeling my baby's movements. I loved that sensation. It was like a miracle, reassuring me that my baby was alive and healthy.

My stomach had grown very large, and I could no longer fit into my regular clothes. Mary, George's sister-in-law, had given me one of her old maternity dresses. It didn't look great on me: it was the wrong size. Mary was much larger than I was, but it was all I had, so I'd washed it every night and put it in the airing cupboard to dry for the following morning. Unfortunately, sometimes it was still slightly wet, and I'd stand before the fire drying it, ready to dash if anyone came down. I longed for the day I'd give birth and could fit back into my regular clothes again.

I always looked forward to my antenatal appointments with Doctor McMullan and kept them all. When he'd ask how everything was going, I'd smile and tell him I was okay. I was too afraid of what George might do to say anything negative about him or his ma. I could tell that Doctor McMullan was not convinced. "If you're worried about anything, Frances, ye can tell me," He'd say. But I'd always reply that everything was fine, and he'd let it go.

A few of George's neighbours had also been asking if I was okay. Perhaps I had been showing signs of the strain I was under. Mrs Murphy, who lived next door, told me to come and visit anytime. She suggested that I might need a chat and some different company. So did another neighbour, a girl called Emma, who lived further up the road. However, Mrs McAteer made it quite clear that she didn't want me talking to any of her neighbours. She suggested that they were all a bunch of nosy fuckers. So, I'd have to wait until she was out before talking with any of them, and I never discussed what went on at home, although I had suspected they had guessed. Although I was depressed, I tried to put on a front for everyone.

Early one July morning, I'd woken and slipped down to the kitchen to get myself a mug of tea before anyone else was up. I took it into the back garden and took a deep breath, trying to rid myself of the stress of the previous night. Once again, George had returned home drunk and forced himself on top of me. It had become routine, and I wondered if this was how it would be for the rest of my life.

I wouldn't say I liked the predicament I was in, and I felt very depressed. I was constantly on my guard and desperately needed something to change. My mind flashed back to my childhood, the farm where the nuns had sent me, and the two men who had sexually abused me. The feelings I had now, whenever George forced himself on me, were the same as when they had molested me. There were times when I'd felt like stabbing George to make it stop. I wasn't sure how long I could hold all these feelings in.

Suddenly, a dog barked, and Max's racing pigeons started cooing loudly, disturbing the peace that I needed to think.

I went back indoors and was startled to see my mother-in-law in the kitchen: she didn't usually get up this early. I felt uncomfortable and wasn't sure how to act in front of her. I noticed that she didn't look comfortable either, seeing me there. Maybe because she was used to having an audience of family members around her, she needed them to be witnesses when welding her authority. It gave her an air of importance. She threw me a dirty look, and I dragged my eyes away from her direction.

"What are you doing, sneaking about like that, Reilly?"

"I wasn't doing anything, and if I was being quiet, it was so as not to disturb anyone. I couldn't sleep, so I came down to make a cup of tea," I answered and walked on past her.

Back in the bedroom, I sat down carefully on the edge of the bed, not wanting to wake George. He didn't stir, and I sat deep in thought for over an hour. It was then that I decided to find somewhere else to live. I couldn't wait any longer for a council house. It was taking too long, and I didn't want to be under Mrs McAteer's roof a moment longer. Also, I had convinced myself that George might change once he was away from her influence.

George woke, disturbing my thoughts, and went downstairs to use the bathroom. I could hear him talking to his mother, and about ten minutes later, he returned to inform me that she and his sister were on their way out. They were going to visit his auntie and would be out all day. While they were out, I was to clean the house from top to bottom. Great, I thought, better a day's cleaning than being stuck with her all day. George left, saying he was just off to see if his dad and brothers wanted to go fly-fishing.

With the family out for the day, I hurriedly tackled the housework. I wanted to finish early, so I'd have time to visit with a few neighbours. It was time to confide in someone, but I was worried it might backfire on me should I talk to the wrong person. I wondered who I could trust, and I felt I needed a sign to guide me. Then, around lunchtime, I saw Emma walking past the house on her way home. My decision was made; this was all the sign I needed to prompt me to action.

I ran to the front door and called her over. She turned towards me, a puzzled expression on her face. "Hello, Frances. Are ye all right?"

"I'm not too good, Emma. Could you come in for a wee chat?" She hesitated. "It's okay, they're all out and won't be back for a while."

Although apprehensive initially, she seemed pleased that I'd asked her in. I made some tea and then poured my heart out to her. It was a relief to have someone to talk to, and I felt like a huge weight had been lifted. Like some of the other neighbours, she told me she'd already guessed that I wasn't happy and offered to help me find somewhere else to live.

"Ye know what it's like around here, Frances. People don't miss a trick, and they'll gossip about anything. They might engage in pleasantries with Mrs McAteer, but they all know what she's like. Some people around here feel sorry for ye."

It was a relief to have someone to talk to, and I took comfort from her words. "Just give me a minute to tell me ma where I am, and then we'll go into town. I saw her out the door and watched her as she dashed towards her front door and then returned indoors to finish the tidying.

Emma and I spent that whole afternoon searching for a cheap flat to rent. We looked at notices in shop windows, read the local newspapers, and then started asking around. Emma stopped everyone she knew, and eventually, a lady gave us an address on Castle Street to try. The man we needed to talk to was Paddy Woods.

We rushed there at once. Castle Street was close to the town centre, and we soon stood outside an old terrace house. It was a rather dull three-story building. The front door and windows appeared to have been painted green but were so dirty it was difficult to be sure. I could tell that Emma was not impressed and wanted to leave at once, but I was desperate. I knocked loudly on the door with the old brass knocker. We waited a few moments, and Emma said we should go. I decided to wait another minute, but there was no response. I knocked again, and this time, we could hear a voice.

"I'm coming; I'm coming." It sounded like an elderly or very sick man. We could hear him fumbling around with the door latch, which eventually opened.

A scruffy man, well into his eighties, stood hunched over, leaning on his walking stick. "What would ye be wanting? I'm not buying anything off, ye," he scolded.

"We were wondering if you had a flat for rent. Mrs Quigly told us to try you because you rent rooms to people," Emma politely inquired.

"Ye better come on in; I can't be standing here for too long," he moaned as he turned slowly and shuffled down the hallway, his voice echoing behind him.

We stepped inside, closed the creaky door, and followed him slowly to the back of the long, narrow house. The prospects inside the hall were even less inviting than those outside. It was dull, dingy and hadn't been cleaned properly for many years. Emma nudged my arm and gestured to the door, suggesting we should leave. I didn't think we should be rude, so I shrugged and followed him into the kitchen. Then, looking at each other, we both got a fit of the giggles. I wasn't sure it was a laughing matter, but it was impossible to keep a straight face once we'd started.

Paddy sat himself down beside the hot range in a tattered and torn armchair. He pointed towards a few wooden chairs and a small foldaway table and asked us to sit. We chatted with him for a short while. He wanted to know who we were and inquired who our families were. That information would inform him if we might be trustworthy or not.

Then, eventually, he told us there was a room at the very top of the house, which I could rent for thirty shillings a week. He asked me to pass him a bunch of keys, tied onto a shoelace and hanging from a hook at the back of the door. They were huge and old, like the ones back at the convent. Removing a large key, he handed it to me. That's going to be hard to fit into my purse, I realised. He couldn't come up the stairs with us as he was unable to manage them. Great, I thought, not because he was frail but it meant he wouldn't be popping up all the time.

The ceilings of the first two floors were tall, with two flights of stairs between each level. At the top of the first flight, before the stairs turned back on themselves, was a tiny landing with a window overlooking a dilapidated backyard. We carried on up the remaining flights of stairs to the top floor. By now, I was struggling and had to stop for a minute to catch my breath. The climb wouldn't have been problematic if I hadn't been pregnant.

Emma took the key from me while I caught my breath. She tried to unlock the door, but the key refused to turn. I could see how hard she was pushing from the pained expression on her face. I gave it a go myself but failed to move it. Neither of us wanted to return downstairs and ask the old man for his help. It had probably been years since he last climbed the stairs, so we struggled until, at last, the key turned with a loud clunking sound. I wondered how long it had been since the door had been unlocked.

Suddenly, the door creaked open, and we peered into the dusty room. It had a damp, musty smell, and it looked as though it had been shut up since the war. It must have been used as a storeroom at some point. Boxes, junk and some old furniture lay entombed in a dense layer of dust and cobwebs.

As we stepped into the room, the dank smell overpowered us, and we covered our mouths with our coat sleeves. The wallpaper and ceiling were stained with large brown and yellow patches of damp, and it was so dirty that it was hard to tell what their original colours had been. On the right-hand wall was an old fireplace with a stone mantelpiece. Above it, attached to the wall, were two old-fashioned gas lamps. I had never seen gas lamps and wondered if they still worked. There wasn't any electricity or running water. Neither of us spoke as we tried to take in what we were looking at. I couldn't believe it. It appeared we had been transported back to another historical period.

The sound of traffic and people talking on the street below drew us to the window, but years of built-up dirt and grime prevented us from seeing out. I pushed hard on the window latch, forcing it to move, and then, with Emma's help, slid open the window. We hung our heads out, breathing in the fresh air and looking down on Castle Street.

"It would be great to live in the town, with the shops just outside the door."

"Please, Frances, tell me you're joking. Ye can't live here. It's awful!" Emma said in disbelief.

I could hardly believe I was considering it myself. Still, I was desperate to get away from Mrs McAteer, and there wasn't anywhere else to rent that was this cheap. "It doesn't look like much now, Emma, but with a lot of hard work and a bit of imagination. I could make it look nice."

I must have sounded convincing, desperate, or both because she put her arm around my shoulder and offered to help. We left the window open to air the room, left the door unlocked because it was clear that nobody ever came up these stairs, and headed back down. I wanted to move in as soon as it could be cleaned up and was eager to get started.

In the kitchen, Paddy told us that the toilet was out in the backyard and that there was also a tap to get water. I'd have to fetch it up the stairs in the bucket. Emma looked at me, horrified at the prospect of hiking up those stairs with buckets of water, especially in my condition. However, having grown up in a convent it didn't put me off. I was well used to hard work and living at Paddy's held more appeal for me than the prospect of remaining at George's house.

We agreed that Paddy would give me a few weeks to clean the room before I moved in and started paying rent. He handed me another key for the front door, and I thanked him and left.

On the way back, Emma said that she could get most of the cleaning items from her house and that maybe a few of the neighbours could help. "Me ma like's ye, Frances, and she'd want to help ye." Now, Mrs McAteer won't catch on when we sneak off to clean the room." I felt very grateful to her for her support. It was great to have a friend I could trust, and for now, we shared this secret.

When I arrived back at the house, I was pleased to see that no one had returned, so they wouldn't even know I'd been out.

George and his brothers came home first. They were in a great mood and looked pleased with the fish they'd caught. I asked where Max was, and George told me his dad hadn't gone fishing. He'd met his friend, Barney, who'd asked him to go to the pub.

 I lay on my bed, thinking about the little room I'd rented and wondering how good it could look when we'd finished. Maybe I was fooling myself into thinking that it could be transformed into a warm, cosy place to live when the dirt and grime were cleaned away. It needed to be nice before I could tell George anything about it. Then, just after seven, I heard Max at the front door. He sounded merry as he chatted with his sons about their day out fishing.

Unfortunately, it wasn't long before Mrs McAteer came home and roared at Max for being in the pub again. I couldn't blame him for that: she would drive anyone away. I'd be in the pub all day if I had to live my life with her.

"Well, I hope you've had your dinner, Max, because there's none for ye here!" she hollered. "Ye can find someone else to cook for ye because I'm not going to. I'm off out, and ye can like it or lump it."

I was sure the whole street must have heard her. The front door slammed shut, then immediately opened again, and now Max was shouting.

"Go on off then and see your fancy man!" he bellowed after her.

Intrigued, this was the first I'd heard that she might have been having an affair. Although, when I gave it more thought, I wasn't surprised.

Soon after that, George and John were back off out for a drink, so I decided to go down and see if Max was all right. There he was, sitting alone in the kitchen, smoking his pipe. He appeared sad and tired as he raised his head and forced a smile.

I filled the kettle and placed it on the gas cooker. "I'll get ye a nice wee cup of tea, Max and some dinner. Are ye hungry?" I said, feeling sorry for him.

"Thanks, Frances. That would be grand. You're a good wee girl," he sighed and relaxed, lying back in his chair.

After scanning the cupboards and fridge, I found some mincemeat, potatoes, carrots and onions and set about preparing a meal. The smell of cooking soon filled the kitchen. As Max sipped his tea, he appeared to be daydreaming as if trying to remember something significant.

When I served Max his dinner, he asked if I would sit and keep him company for a while. I felt very sorry for him and was pleased he'd invited me. He looked worn out! Pulling a chair out from the table, I sat down opposite him.

He took a few mouthfuls of his dinner and said it tasted delicious. I was glad then that Mr McConnell's sister had taught me a lot about cooking. She had written books on the subject and had taught cooking at a college in Southern Ireland.

"I don't think I've told ye, Frances, but I knew your mother; you remind me of her. You're the image of her when she'd have been about your age."

Shocked, I didn't know what to say. It was a complicated subject for me because I had no memories of my mother before she left my sisters and me, at the age of two, with the nuns at Nazareth House in Belfast. Almost all that I knew about her was what my aunt had told me, and none of that had been pleasant to listen to. Perhaps Max guessed what I was thinking because he told me not to be so hard on her. He seemed to be sure that she had her reasons for what she did concerning me and my sisters. I didn't feel like being that forgiving, but I kept silent and just let him talk.

"She was wild and a free spirit who never conformed to what others expected of her, and this got her into a lot of trouble, even with her family. She was an embarrassment to them." He told me that she didn't seem to care about anything or anyone. He'd been intrigued by her for a long time and eventually fell in love with her. I didn't expect to hear this, and it shocked me, making me freeze on the spot. I found it hard to grasp what he was telling me, but I knew he was being honest.

He stopped to eat some more of his dinner, then, after a brief pause, he continued. My eyes were fixed on him now, wanting him to continue his story. "I asked your mother to marry me three times, and each time she refused. The last time, I told her I wouldn't ask her again. Soon after her last refusal, I married my wife. She always knew I was on the rebound from your mother. "I'm sorry, Frances, but this is why my wife can't deal with you in the family. Ye know, ye do look just like her."

This revelation shocked me, especially as it was clear that he still had fond memories and strong feelings for my mother. He went on to tell me more about when they were young. His face lit up, remembering it all, and it appeared to be doing him some good. I couldn't help laughing at the things they had gotten up to. She was wild!

One time, when my mother was about fifteen and all her family were at Sunday mass, she took the mattresses off their beds. She piled them up in the middle of the street and poured paraffin all over them. Then, when she saw them walking back down the road, she set fire to them and ran off. No wonder my aunts hated her.

Finally, I understood why Mrs McAteer hated me with such a passion and that there was nothing I could do to change her perception of me!

Moving in Day

Over the next few weeks, armed with a mop, bucket and as many cleaning products as her mum could spare, Emma and I went on a cleaning mission, visiting the bedsit as often as possible. I used every excuse in the book to escape from the house without anyone noticing what I was getting up to. This morning's excuse was an appointment at the county hospital. I knew nobody would be interested in attending the appointment with me so I could safely be away from the house for several hours. Emma met me outside the shop just as we'd arranged, and we hurried down the Derry Road, talking and laughing along the way.

Both Emma and I were buzzing with excitement as we witnessed the transformation taking place in my modest rented room. I eagerly anticipated my liberation from the confines of George's family home. Following Paddy Woods's advice, we had been diligent in clearing out the clutter. We were relegating unwanted items to an empty room. With most of the junk removed, we focused on revitalising the space and retaining only essential furnishings: a sturdy iron bed, a compact cupboard for provisions, a weathered wardrobe, and a well-loved armchair, which we meticulously scrubbed and polished to restore its former lustre.

As our efforts progressed, we became increasingly ambitious. Next, we turned our attention to the fabric of the room. We painstakingly cleaned and polished the windows to a gleaming shine. Stripped away the worn wallpaper to reveal the bare walls beneath. Even the fireplace, once neglected and grimy, underwent a remarkable transformation under our diligent scrubbing. The lino floor had already been scrubbed three times and a pattern was now becoming visible, but it would need more work before we could see the design more clearly.

Resourceful as ever, we managed to rustle up paint for the walls, harbouring hopes that a fresh coat would brighten up the room,. Though our task was far from complete, the gradual metamorphosis of the space filled us with a sense of accomplishment and eager anticipation.

I had confided in my friends Paddy and Mrs McConnell about the room, knowing I could trust them. Paddy would meet us there today with a paintbrush and some paint, which his dad said I was most welcome to. Paddy said he would paint the walls as it wouldn't take too long with the small size of the place. Mrs McConnell said she would help me with some essentials when I finished the room.

I was out of breath and glad to reach the top of the stairs. My stomach was enormous now and I could feel my baby moving and kicking most of the time. I would only have to wait another few weeks for the birth. As I rested against the wall, momentarily, Emma touched my stomach to feel the baby's movement. Her face glowed with surprise as the baby obliged with one movement after another.

"Oh, Frances, it's wonderful. I can't wait to see the baby when it's born. I wonder if it will look like you."

"I can't wait until it's born either, Emma. If it gets much bigger, I won't be able to walk anywhere. I've been wanting to ask ye if you'd be the baby's godmother. I can't think of anyone else I'd rather have."

Emma looked positively shocked, and, for a moment, I thought she might burst into tears. "Oh my God, really, Frances, I would love to!"

I knew she would be a great godmother. I felt tremendously happy to have her as a true friend. We let ourselves into the room and sat down for a short rest.

Munching through some fruit shortcake biscuits, we began discussing babies' names again. As usual, I didn't bother to mention any boy's name as I felt certain it would be a girl. It had never occurred to me that it wouldn't be a girl. Whenever Emma said a boy's name, I would instantly dismiss it.

"Frances, what if ye have a boy? Wouldn't ye need a boy's name, just in case?" she asked me.

"No, it's going to be a girl; I just know it," I replied. Emma gave me a strange look but said no more on the subject.

Determined to reveal more of the floor pattern, we began scrubbing the floor again. It was hard to believe that there was still more dirt coming off. As we worked, girls' names filled my mind. I still hadn't settled on one and felt I should have one ready before the baby was born.

Paddy arrived, smiling as cheerfully as ever, in shabby work clothes with a paintbrush stuck out from his back pocket. He was holding a large tin of paint. Some of the paint had run down the side of the tin and dried. It was a beautiful daffodil-yellow shade, and I thought it would be a calming colour for my child. That caused me to smile, thinking it would be just right to brighten up the dreary-looking walls.

"Where do ye want me to start?" asked Paddy, eager to help.

"Wherever ye want, Paddy, sure, I don't know anything about painting. Anyway, thanks for your help. I do appreciate ye given your time. That yellow should brighten this room nicely," Paddy opened the can while I returned to scrubbing the floor. Time was precious, and we didn't want to waste a second of it. Each achievement brought me much closer to being free from Mrs McAteer.

"Just think, Frances, I can visit anytime. It will be great." Paddy was excited for me to have this little place of my own. It was good to have Paddy around, as he always seemed to cheer me up. He whistled, sang, and told us ghost stories while we worked, which helped us to keep going and stay in high spirits.

At last, the room was done. The floor looked as good as we could get it, and if we scrubbed any harder, there was a danger of us boring a hole in the lino. The paint had brightened the place up. It still looked small - we could do nothing about that - but it was no longer dark and dingy. The clean bed and polished wardrobe and chair were in place, so all that was needed now was a cooker plus a few things to make it more homely. We opened the window to remove the paint fumes and locked the door.

Butterflies filled my stomach as I walked back to the house. I knew I couldn't put it off any longer and had to tell George about my plan to move out. I wasn't sure how he would react. He might be furious, and maybe he wouldn't want to move. After all, he wasn't the one who had a problem living there.

When we reached the phone, box near George's house, I stopped to call Mrs McConnell. She sounded pleased when I told her that we had finished the room.

"Have ye informed his lordship yet?" she asked, sounding concerned about me.

"No, not yet. I'm going to the gas shop tomorrow to see if I can pay weekly for a cooker. Once I've got that, I'll tell him, and he can come and look at the room with me."

She asked if he would be okay with me doing all this without telling him. "I don't know," I told her. "He would never have agreed to it if I had asked him beforehand, not while the room was in that awful state."

"Well, he can always stay with his mother if he doesn't like it," I suggested. "That would suit me." I wouldn't be staying in that house any longer than I had to. I was determined and knew no one could talk me out of it. This move was happening whether George liked it or not.

"Can you be at your new place tomorrow afternoon, Frances, at about three o'clock so I can come up and have a look at it?" she inquired. Then she told me that she'd sorted out a few bits and pieces which she thought may be useful for me. I thanked her and told her that sounded grand.

When I told Emma what Mrs McConnell said, I realised I'd need another excuse for tomorrow afternoon. We sat on the little wall by the phone box, trying to think of one. After many foolish ideas from both of us, Emma suggested I tell them I had to return to the hospital for a blood test. When I got home, fortunately, no one was interested in how things had gone at the hospital. I was grateful for that, as I would have had to lie again. It occurred to me that if the nuns were right about lying, I would almost certainly be going to hell!

Up in the bedroom, I pondered how to tell George. Could this be the making of us? I wondered. Would he change once he was away from his family and once the baby was born? We could be like a proper family then. However, even as I was thinking this, I knew deep down that he wouldn't change. Even if he promised and swore on the bible, nothing would change. The fact that I cringed every time he touched me wasn't going to change how I felt. I think it made him feel inadequate, but I couldn't get over it. Anyway, at least I would be away from his mother.

The following day, my twenty-five-pound maternity grant arrived in the post. Fortunately, I had been expecting it and got to the letters before anyone else was up. I hid it in my pocket until I could cash it at the post office. George would have gone to the pub with the money if he had known about it.

Once he was up, he told me he was going fishing for the day with his brothers. When I said I had to return to the hospital for blood tests he groaned, "Ye, okay," completely disinterested.

As soon as he got downstairs, I could hear Mrs McAteer moaning, wanting to know if I was coming down to clean up as I should be earning my keep. When George told her I had to return to the hospital for something, she insisted I should, "Bloody well clean up first."

As she had to go into town, George came up and passed the message on.

"I'll do it in a wee while. I've got morning sickness," I explained. George left the room to sort out the fishing gear. I felt highly pleased with myself for arranging somewhere else to live; I could no longer endure living in the same house as that woman.

The main post office was packed, and the queues were long and slow-moving. My legs and back ached, and I was still nauseous and somewhat uncomfortable. The baby was kicking a lot, and I was relieved when it was finally my turn. I felt rich walking out of the post office with my twenty-five pounds. It was the largest amount of money I'd ever held, and I rushed off to the gas shop.

The man in the gas shop explained that I could get a new gas cooker for five shillings per week. He could deliver it today with a new gas bottle. I was delighted that, finally, I was taking control of my situation. The shop was just across the road from Paddy's, so they wouldn't have far to go. They didn't seem bothered when I told them it was at the top of the house. I was delighted and paid up a few months in advance. Next, I headed to the bakery and bought myself the most enormous fresh cream cake. Then, I rushed over to my new home to enjoy it.

Paddy Woods was sitting in his kitchen, warming himself by the range. "Hello, Paddy. How are ye?' I inquired.

"Well, now Frances. When ye get old, ye always feel the cold more. It's hard work trying to keep warm," he said, forcing a smile.

I was thinking about his life and didn't suppose he had much to look forward to or smile about. It appears he was just sitting about, waiting to die.

"Here's two months' rent for ye Paddy. Now, can I make ye a wee cup of tea?" The money and tea seemed to cheer him up a little bit, and we talked for a while.

"Thank you, that's grand, Frances. Now I'll just sort out a wee rent book and sign this in." Paddy rose from his chair with deliberate movements, making his way to a cupboard while I tended to his kettle, placing it on top of the range to heat. Returning to his seat, Paddy produced a small rent book and a pencil. His hand trembled slightly as he recorded the payment I had made, his signature a testament to his effort.

Observing his frailty, I couldn't help but feel a pang of sympathy for Paddy. His solitary existence, marked by the daily struggle to keep warm and carry out even the simplest tasks, weighed heavily upon me. As I rinsed the tea leaves from the pot, I resolved to brighten his days whenever possible, vowing to visit him for a chat and offer him a cup of tea as a token of companionship.

It was strange opening the door to my room and seeing the bright yellow walls, the clean floor, the shiny fireplace, and the sparkling windows. It was my first time alone in the room without having any cleaning to do. I sat down on the armchair and began eating my cream cake. Even though I could hear the traffic and people talking on the street below me, it felt peaceful.

For the first time, I felt I had a place that was mine; my first real home. There were no nuns or Mrs McAteer to boss me about, no ringing bells, no rules about how I should behave and when I had to be in. I hadn't realised, until then, how much joy I'd gotten out of transforming the room into a home. I didn't want to share it with George or anyone except my baby. I wasn't looking forward to telling George because, even if he wanted to move in, it wouldn't feel like my tiny home anymore.

I was finishing my delicious cake when I heard a loud knock on the front door. I rushed down and opened it, and two delivery men were waiting with my new cooker, which was still covered in plastic.

"Hello, Frances, is it? Where do you want this cooker placed?"

"I'm right up at the top of the stairs" I replied. I hadn't seen these two men in the shop, and I was hoping that they wouldn't mind taking it all the way up for me. They didn't seem to mind, and I followed them up, feeling excited. I couldn't wait to see it in my room once all the plastic had been removed. I imagined myself cooking on it and was glad I could now have a cup of tea in my room.

When Mrs McConnell arrived, she was carrying two large boxes, which she placed on the bed. Then she returned to her car for a small fold-up table, and back down again for the rest. She couldn't stay long and hoped that what she'd brought would be helpful. Before she left, she admired the new cooker and all the work that had gone into the room to make it nice. "I hope you'll be very happy here, Frances. You've done a grand job, and you should be very proud of yourself. I'm amazed, Frances, I think you could make a home out of anything." I thanked her and watched as she disappeared down the stairs.

The boxes contained sheets and pillowcases, curtains, saucepans, a teapot, dishcloths, tea towels, hand towels, bath towels, tablecloths, mugs, plates, a lovely vase, and knives, and forks. While the bags held all manner of groceries, including sugar, tea, bread, milk, rice, tinned goods and fresh vegetables. I felt overwhelmed by Mrs

McConnell's kindness, and, with all the emotion I was feeling, my eyes began to well up with tears.

Then I noticed an envelope in one of the bags. When I opened it, I saw a cheque made out to me for twenty pounds and a card congratulating me on my new home. Written inside the card was a note, "To Frances, this money is for you and the baby. Please don't let his lordship get his hands on it, your friend, Mrs E. McConnell."

When people are kind to me, it usually results in me not knowing how to respond and wondering why they were being so nice to me. A lifetime of abuse had normalised the cruelty, and I could deal with the cruelty much more easily than people being kind. I couldn't understand why somebody like Mrs McConnell would be so thoughtful and caring to someone like me. After all, I didn't work for her anymore, and she shouldn't have felt obliged to help me this much. I'd been treated like a nobody for so long that it was how I felt most of the time. I wiped my tears away and told myself to stop being so stupid.

I looked again at all she had brought me and began thinking about how I could make use of everything. She had told me that she would sort out a few things that she no longer had a use for, but I couldn't help but notice how everything looked brand new like it had come straight from the shops. I found a space for the little fold-up table and covered it with a white linen tablecloth. I placed the vase in the middle - I would get a few flowers to put in later. The flannelette sheets felt soft and warm as I held them to my face before putting them on the old iron bed with its horsehair mattress, which was rock hard. I decided to put one of the blankets that Paddy would be bringing later from his mother's house under the sheet to make the bed softer and more comfortable. I felt so thankful to Paddy and his family, too, for providing me with a few pillows and blankets. That was all I needed for us to move in. I was ready, and I felt empowered to take my life back.

The front door knocked again, and I rushed to see who it was, but I could hear that they had already been let in. Footsteps quickened on the stairs, and I could see the top of Emma's head as she approached the last flight. I wasn't expecting to see her, so it was a pleasant surprise.

"How are ye getting on?" she asked as she arrived at the top.

"I've got my cooker and Mrs McConnell has been to visit with some things. Come on in, Emma, and have a wee look." I couldn't hide my excitement and wanted to show her everything at once. She was so happy for me; she reached out to me and gave me the biggest hug.

"Oh, Frances! I love the cooker and everything. It looks so different here now. Ye, wouldn't believe it was the same wee room we first came into just a few weeks ago."

"Yeah, I know, and thanks to you for helping me, Emma. Let's go to the Golden Griddle, and I will treat ye." When I told her about the money I had received today, she agreed.

We didn't have far to walk and enjoyed eating and catching up on everything. "I guess that now the room is almost done, I'm going to have to tell George about it." She agreed and said she would keep her fingers crossed for me so he wouldn't get angry.

When Emma had to leave, I returned to my little room with some things I had bought in town to finish it off. I was getting stuck in, trying to make it as homely as possible, when Paddy arrived at my door, smiling.

He told me the front door hadn't been closed properly, so he let himself in. Paddy Woods had already warned me of that - complaining that the people who lived under me often left it open. I was pleased to see Paddy and show him the room now that it was almost finished. He was very impressed, knowing what it had been like.

Paddy had brought a few lagers with him and had just started one. "These drinks are for celebrating," he said. "I know ye don't drink Frances but maybe just a wee bit in a glass to toast your new place." I was excited about getting away from George's mum and readily agreed.

We'd been chatting for a while when Paddy asked me about George. "To be honest, Paddy, I've been thinking about whether I should just move in alone and not tell him." Paddy choked on his lager and thought I must be joking.

"Ye had me going for a wee minute there, Frances. Now, don't ye scare me like that again? Ye know that George would do his nut."

"If I moved out of the house tonight, it wouldn't be too soon."

"Well, ye could move out tonight; ye just need to tell George! There's nothing else stopping ye, come on, I'll help ye get the last few wee bits sorted.

I began stacking the food into a small cupboard while Paddy went down to the backyard to fill four big plastic buckets full of water, which he placed in the hallway outside my door. I'd just bought them in the hardware shop along with plastic covers to place over them. I took a jug and got some water to make our first pot of tea.

After one final trip to the shops for coal and firelighters, all that was left to do was hang the curtains. They were yellow with a thin green stripe running through them, and they framed the window beautifully, adding to that homely feeling I was aiming for. Now, the room was finally finished and ready to move into.

I felt sick on the way back, and my stomach wouldn't settle. I was worried about George but was truly terrified at the thought of how Mrs McAteer would react. After all, she would lose her skivvy and have no one but Max left to whinge at. I had envied him at times, being able to walk out and leave her to get on with it. I wished, as hard as I could, that George would be in a good mood when I got in. I desperately needed him to be pleased about the bedsit. George wasn't home, and his youngest brother Ed told me he'd gone to the pub. They were delighted with what they had caught while fishing, and John said he would buy the pints. I felt frustrated, having finally psyched myself up to talk to him. Unfortunately, Mrs McAteer was in her usual foul mood and complaining about everything.

"Reilly, ye can peel those spuds and carrots for dinner." She pointed to the pile of vegetables stacked up on the draining board in the kitchen. "Also, tomorrow morning, Reilly, ye can clean the house from top to bottom. I'm not fucking giving ye charity while you're here." I could feel my blood boiling in anger, and I stormed off into the kitchen. I lifted the knife and began peeling the veg, consoling myself by thinking that I wouldn't have to be there much longer.

Ed entered the kitchen and whispered, "She had another argument with me, da, and he stormed off to join George at the pub." Ed felt sorry for me, having to endure his mother's bullshit. She wouldn't have been too happy if she'd seen him whispering to me. He took himself back into the living room, holding a glass of water, trying to make it look as though that was what he had gone to the kitchen for.

I thought how ridiculous it was that everyone crept around Mrs McAteer, afraid of upsetting this woman when she didn't seem to care about anybody's feelings but her own. Frustration had built up inside me, and my blood was boiling. I felt like I might explode and wanted to leave the house now! I wished I had the nerve to pack my bag and walk out without saying a word.

There was a knock at the front door, and Mrs McAteer went to answer it; it was one of the neighbours. They stopped on the doorstep for a bit of gossip, and I could hear the woman telling Mrs McAteer that she'd seen me, with Emma, in the town. "They seem to be such good friends. Did she buy something nice for the baby?" the nosy woman inquired.

"She's a lying wee bitch, that one! She told George she was at the hospital," Mrs McAteer replied. It was clear from her tone that she was ready for an argument.

"Sounds like you're in trouble!" Ed whispered, clearly concerned.

"I've got somewhere to live, Ed, but don't tell your ma. Tell George to come to 10 Castle Street if I storm out of here before he gets back."

"Does George know ye were looking for somewhere 'cause he didn't say anything to us? Mind you, I don't blame ye. I'd get out of here too, if I were you. It won't get any easier for ye here even after ye have the wee baby."

"Thanks for understanding, Ed. No, George doesn't know yet. I was going to surprise him tonight."

"Oh my God, Frances, it will be a surprise, all right. I don't think George was even thinking of moving out," he said with a cheeky grin.

I'd finished peeling the potatoes and was starting on the carrots when Mrs McAteer stormed into the kitchen.

"And just what were you doing in town with Emma? Weren't ye supposed to be at the hospital," she raged. "Meeting up with some boys again, I bet. Well, we'll see what George makes of this, when I tell him you've been galloping about the town all day like some brazen hussy."

That did it for me: I was so sick of this woman. I lost my temper and howled at her. "We're not all like you; we all know what you get up to behind Max's back. It's none of your fucking business what I do and who I hang around with." I snapped back at her. My whole body was shaking with anger.

Ed jumped to his feet, unsure what to do and worried what would happen next. His mouth gaped open in disbelief. He wasn't used to seeing anyone stand up to his ma like that, especially me.

Mrs McAteer's face turned crimson. She rushed towards me and slapped me hard across my face. "Don't you bloody dare speak to me like that, ye wee bitch," she screeched.

I wanted to stab her with the knife I was holding, but I threw it down in the sink instead and ran past her, grabbing my coat and bag along the way. She was still screaming when I was off out of the front door, making sure to slam it hard behind me. I kept running until I had reached the shops where there were people around outside. Only then did I looked back to see if she was following, but she wasn't, so I stopped to catch my breath and take in all that had happened back at the house.

Although I was shaken and felt furious, it was also a relief to be out of there. I finally told her how I felt about her, and it was invigorating. Also, she had saved me from having to tell George about the room. Emma had the key to my bedsit so I would have to get it from her. She would be shocked about me rebelling like that, but there was no way I could return to that awful house now.

By the time I'd got to Emma's, my anger had turned to tears, and the side of my face was burning from the slap.

"Hello, Frances, what's wrong? Come on in," Emma's mother said, putting her arm around me. "Are ye all right now, Frances? What the hell has happened?"

Emma must have heard her mother because she came rushing downstairs to see what was happening. They were very sympathetic and understanding as I explained everything. "I don't blame ye for running out, Frances. I would have done the same thing." Emma exclaimed. She put the kettle on for a cup of tea while her mother made some ham sandwiches. I wasn't hungry, but she insisted I keep my strength up for the baby's sake.

"Emma, will ye go with, Frances, to the bedsit? Keep her company for a wee while, and I'll get ye a lift home later," her mother insisted.

I thanked Emma's mother for being so understanding. Then we left by the back door and headed to my new home.

Although it was a relief not to be returning to that house again, I still feared George's reaction. What had just happened with Mrs McAteer wasn't going to help the situation. Hopefully, Ed would get to him first before she riled him. Emma asked me to tell her what happened all over again. She enjoyed hearing how I stood up to Mrs McAteer. As I repeated the words, I found the funny side of it all, and we laughed as we walked down the road.

When I thought about what Mrs McAteer might be doing now, I thought of Ed, who was alone in the house with her. "Oh my god, Emma, she's probably going mental and doing Ed's head in. He'll have to put up with all her moaning until George gets back."

Emma laughed and said, "Well, ye can't help that, Frances. I'm sure he knows what she's like. Maybe he'll even get a wee kick out of it. It's not often people stand up to that old witch."

We had called in at a shop on Castle Street for some candles and matches as there was no electricity on the top floor. I wasn't sure if the two gas lights on the wall worked, but as soon as we'd let ourselves in, we decided to check them out. When I put a match to them, we were both shocked to see that they still worked. However, from all the smoke, it was apparent that the mantles needed replacing. I hoped we could find a shop that still sold them. I wasn't sure how long-ago people used gaslights, but they seemed archaic.

We made some tea and got ourselves comfortable. It was great being in my new home and having Emma stay for a while. We talked for hours, and I hoped George wouldn't turn up. Maybe he would take his mother's side and stay there. A part of me knew that was only wishful thinking. If he was going to come to the new place, then I hoped it would be soon. He would never make a fuss while Emma was still there. He wouldn't shout at me in front of people, that wasn't his way. He preferred waiting until I was on my own because he wanted people to think he was such a nice bloke. I wanted time to explain everything to him before he got into a temper with me.

At around eleven o'clock, there was a knock on the front door, and Emma ran down to see who it was. She returned, saying it was her lift and that she would call in tomorrow to see how I was, and then she disappeared back downstairs. Sitting in the quiet candlelit room, I wasn't sure what to do with myself now and wondered if George would turn up or stay home. One thing was certain: I wouldn't be able to sleep until I found out what was happening back at his house.

The hours passed slowly, and I worked myself up into a stressed state of mind. Finally, in the early hours, I heard George's voice from outside on the street shouting.

"Frances, are ye in there?" He was shouting through the letterbox, and it was clear that he was even drunker than usual. I dashed downstairs quickly before the racket awoke Paddy. When I opened the door, I found him propped up against the wall in a heap, hardly able to stand. I held him up, as best I could, and tried to get him to walk.

Getting him up the stairs was a slow and gruelling process: I had to keep stopping for a rest. My stomach ached, and the baby's weight along with George, was too much for me to carry. When I eventually got him into the room and was able to let go; he collapsed into a heap on the floor, his eyes shut tight.

The smell of alcohol quickly filled the room and made me feel nauseous. I undid his shoelaces and placed the washing-up basin beside him. I put a pillow under his head. He just lay there, an unconscious heap in the centre of the floor. I made another cup of tea and sat in the armchair, feeling overtired and very uncomfortable.

My baby was moving about, kicking my already painful stomach, and I wondered if I'd gone into labour. I couldn't be sure. I had no idea what childbirth would feel like, and I told myself to stay calm and breathe deeply. Exhausted, I fell asleep, curled up on the armchair.

By the time I woke to the sound of traffic, my body was cramped and stiff. George was still sleeping noisily on the floor. Quietly, I got up and crept downstairs to the backyard to go to the toilet. It was disgusting and wouldn't flush. I felt sick and had to return to the fresh air before I threw up. I would have to clean it up before George woke up and saw it. Paddy was too old to take care of the place or even care about what state it was in.

I crept back up and got some bleach and clothes. It took nearly a whole bottle of bleach and much elbow grease to make any impact. The stench made me feel sick which was the last thing I needed on top of my morning sickness.

When I returned to the room, George was sitting on the edge of the bed, his head in his hands, groaning. I made him a cup of coffee and told him to drink it. He sipped it slowly and began to come around. The expression on his face changed suddenly as his eyes scanned the room. I realised then that he had no idea where he was or how he'd got there.

"Where the fucking hell are we, Frances, and what the fuck are we doing here?" he demanded. I was in for a struggle; it was going to take more than a new home to change him.

My Beautiful Daughter

The first morning in our new home set the tone for what was to come. George exploded in fury upon learning that I had secured alternative accommodation, without informing him, and he was enraged by the way I had spoken to his mother. His anger soon turned into violence as he lashed out, slapping and punching me before storming back out to the pub. When he woke the following morning, the same argument repeated itself and George was off back down the pub again!

Then, a few days later, he found out about cashing my maternity grant. Unfortunately, his uncle had seen me in the post office, and word had got back to George. Fortunately, by then, I'd spent most of the money on essentials for the baby, which didn't suit him. He told me that I was his wife now, and if he found out I was keeping anything from him again, he would let me have it. I knew exactly what he meant and that he meant it.

Nevertheless, despite all the arguing, I didn't regret, for one moment, the move. I still considered that my life was much better now than when I'd had to put up with his mother, whom I'd not seen since the night I'd stormed out. The sheer relief of escaping her suffocating presence eclipsed any hardships I faced in our new home. That was indeed a blessing!

A month had passed since our move into the bedsit, and any lingering hope I harboured of George changing had all but evaporated. Our interactions had dwindled to near nonexistence, with him absent for most of the day, returning only in the late hours or early mornings. I assumed that he divided most of his time between his mother's house and the pub, seeking refuge there from the responsibilities of home life. When he was drunk, it had become a real struggle to get him upstairs, especially so as my pregnancy progressed. By now, we rarely spoke except to argue.

I was now full term with my pregnancy, and each day I wondered if this would be the day. My stomach was so large that I couldn't see my feet when I stood up, and I had to roll out of bed because I couldn't sit upright. I felt like a beached whale and was suffering severely from backache, heartburn, and sickness. Also, the smell of coffee and fried meat made me feel sick, and I'd cry for no reason.

Emma's mother told her that my hormones were all messed up and that George probably wasn't helping. I was already several weeks late and needed this pregnancy to be over. It was the second day of September, hot and sunny. I'd had enough of sitting in and decided to go out for a long walk and to get some fresh air. In town, I looked in the shop windows at things I dreamed of having but couldn't afford. Most of the money we got subsidised George's drinking habit, and I had found it hard to buy food.

That was okay for him as he could always get something to eat at his mother's house. He didn't seem to care if his drinking meant that the baby and I went without. I'd been living mainly on tea and toast, as there was rarely anything else in the cupboards.

"Hello, Frances," a voice behind me said as I stared at the beautiful baby's cot in the shop window.

"Oh, hello, Mary," I replied as I turned to see my sister-in-law with her daughter, Lilly, asleep in her pram. She looked pleased to see me, claiming she was on her way home, and asked me to return with her for a cup of tea and a sandwich. I took her up on her offer. I needed some food, and a sandwich would be welcome. She strolled along at my pace.

"You look huge, Frances. Are ye sure it's not twins you're carrying?"

"I don't think so, Mary, but I'll be glad when it's all over, just so long as the baby is healthy. That's all I want right now, but getting my figure back will also be great."

Mary usually wore her long, ginger hair tied back. Today, it was down, and she held onto it now and then to prevent it from blowing all over her face. It seemed that she was deliberately trying to cover her left eye. It didn't take me long to figure out why. George and his brother had something in common I thought: they liked to hit their women.

I didn't say anything as she seemed convinced she'd covered it well, and I didn't want to embarrass her. I assumed she would tell me if she wanted to confide in me. The tea, sandwiches and cake were just what I needed along with the conversation. Seeing little Lilly awake, crawling around and pulling herself up on the furniture was beautiful. Watching her made me wonder what my child would look like. Mary and I chatted about what had happened at Mrs McAteer's house, and she agreed that I was better off out of it.

"How's it going with George then, Frances? Are ye happy?" Well, that did it, with everything that had happened, I was at the end of my tether. I needed to talk, but I couldn't be sure she wouldn't tell George's brother, who would then tell his mother. I burst into tears, sobbing uncontrollably, and couldn't speak. I would be glad when my hormones were back to normal. Mary got me some toilet roll and sat beside me to hug me.

"Is this your hormones, Frances or is something wrong with your marriage?"

"Both, I think, Mary. But please don't tell George I said anything to ye. Will you promise me, Mary?" She swore she wouldn't say a word and then pulled back her hair to show me her black and blue swollen eye.

"This is what Jimmy did last night because the dinner wasn't on the table when he got home. It was still cooking, so I told him it would be another ten minutes. He went mad, wrecking the house and beating the shit out of me. If my family knew what he was like, they'd confront him. I know that it would cause a war between our families." Mary looked relieved to be able to tell someone about Jimmy. Despite what he'd done, she loved him and blamed Mrs McAteer for how he was.

"We just have to get on with it, Frances. What else can we do anyway? We're Catholics. We can't divorce."

"Mary, I wish I'd never married George; I should have just taken my chances on my own. It couldn't be worse than this. I don't even like him." She left the room and returned with a mug of hot tea.

"Maybe George will change once the baby's born," she said, handing me the cup. I didn't think she believed that: having her little daughter hadn't changed Jimmy. She was just trying to make me feel better.

I'd been getting pains in my stomach for a while and stood up for a minute to stretch my legs. I assumed the pain had been brought on by all the upset and crying. I didn't realise I might be in labour until I noticed Mary was looking at her watch every time I got one. When she told me my pains were five minutes apart, I panicked. I wasn't sure what having a baby would be like. No one had told me much about that. I'd thought a lot about what it would feel like to hold my baby in my arms, but I had not thought about how it would be born. For someone who grew up like me, it would never have been talked about, and I had been much to embarrassed to ask.

"Oh my god, Mary, will the pain get any worse than this?"

"You're doing fine, Frances, and everyone's different. Some suffer, and some have it easy. Now, I think I'd better call the doctor. I'll have to leave ye a wee minute while I go to the phone box," she said, grabbing her purse and running out of the back door.

Doctor McMullan told Mary to get me to the county hospital immediately, so she'd asked a neighbour to give us a lift. He drove like a lunatic, going through a red light and overtaking traffic on the bends. Mary asked him to slow down as he was scaring us, but he said he didn't want the baby to be born in his car. I was being tossed about on the back seat and was surprised that I hadn't already given birth. It was a tremendous relief to arrive at the hospital in one piece.

"Do ye want me to find George for ye? He'd want to know," she asked. "Not just yet Mary. I don't want to see him yet," I pleaded. There was another excruciating pain, and a nurse sat me down in a wheelchair and told me to relax and take deep breaths with the pain. Mary gave them my details and told me she'd have to get home while I was taken off to the delivery room.

Nine o'clock that evening, I gave birth to my baby girl. It had been a difficult birth, with the cord wrapped around her neck. I barely saw her before they rushed her away. It was worrying, but even more worrying was when I got a glimpse of her being rushed out of the delivery room. I saw that she was black. Although I'd only seen her briefly, I knew what my eyes had seen. I wasn't prejudiced against black people, but she was my daughter. I'd have loved her no matter what colour she was. I couldn't understand how she could be black when her father and I were white. The problem was that George would go mad and say it wasn't his child. It was his child; he was the only person I'd ever been with since leaving the convent.

I was taken to a ward with eight beds. I was given the first bed on the left: all the other beds were taken. The lady in the next bed offered me some chocolate and told me not to look so worried. Then she asked if I'd had a boy or a girl.

"A wee girl, but she's black, and I don't know why 'cause me and my husband are white," I told her. "I have never been with anyone else." I began sobbing. She asked, "Are ye sure your wee girl is black." I told her that I'd seen her with my own eyes. She gave me a concerned look but said nothing.

One of the other women came back into the ward. "Have ye just had a wee girl?" she asked me. I told her I had, and she said she had just come from the nursery and said, "Your daughter is so beautiful. I thought the lady was trying to be kind by not mentioning my child's colour.

The following morning, a nurse arrived in the ward with three babies in her arms. She approached my bed. "Time to see if ye can get your baby to feed from your breast," she announced. "Can ye tell which one is yours?" she asked, smiling at me, assuming that every mother would recognise her own child.

"None of them are mine because my daughter is black," I whispered, not wanting the others in the ward to hear.

She looked at me with a shocked expression. "Did ye have your baby last night?"

"Yeah, I did, and she was black," I said. I didn't want to end up with someone else's baby. I'd heard of things like that happening to other mothers. She walked around the ward, giving the other women their babies, and said she would find out what had happened with my child.

Later, she returned with a doctor who wanted to know why I thought my baby was black. When I explained, he laughed and sat on the edge of my bed. Then he explained that my baby wasn't black. The colour she was at birth resulted from the cord being around her neck for some time. Her colour is back to normal now, he explained. I felt foolish, especially when the lady in the next bed smiled at me.

The nurse came in and placed my baby into my arms. I was overwhelmed with joy at this little child I'd brought into the world. To me, she was perfect, and the woman who had seen her in the nursery was correct. She was so beautiful. I couldn't take my eyes off her. I bonded straight away and immediately wanted to protect her from everything horrible in this world. I wouldn't be able to bear it if she'd had to endure anything as terrible as my sisters and I had to. I closed my eyes and begged the universe to make her life so much more different and better than mine. She was so fragile, and my love for her was immense.

Visiting time came, and everyone had visitors except me. I scanned each visitor as they entered the door, thinking Mary must have told George by now. I figured that he would want to see his daughter, but he didn't show. I should have known this would happen; being the only one without a visitor was embarrassing. It took me back to when I was very young in the convent, looking out for a visitor every Sunday, but no one ever came. I was jealous them of the other girls as most of them knew their family would be there every week. I saddened me to think that my own child was destined to be let down in her life by her father.

Margaret, the lady in the next bed, introduced her family to me. They were a lovely family, and I imagine they must have felt sorry for me, including me in their conversations and coming over to see my baby. They offered me sweets and some magazines, making visiting time more pleasant for me. I was embarrassed to accept their kindness and couldn't understand why I was the only one without visitors at this time.

The rest of the day passed quickly, and I had no problems caring for my baby. Margaret was a lot older than me and struggled nervously with her baby. She commented on how natural I was at caring for mine and was surprised with me being just a teenager. She said not all women can get the hang of babies so quickly. I helped her when she couldn't get the nappy pin through her baby's nappy. I felt proud of myself and was sure my instincts would be enough to make me a good mother.

Visiting time in the evenings was just for husbands, and George was the only one who didn't turn up. I felt embarrassed in front of all the other women and their husbands and pretended to be asleep until the visit was over. The other women got hugs, kisses, flowers and chocolates before their husbands left.

I felt envious of them. That was the sort of husband I would have liked, but all the good things appeared to happen to other people. Perhaps that's why I couldn't believe I'd had such a perfect daughter. She was the best thing that had happened to me, and I knew I probably wouldn't be able to sleep with the excitement of having her with me.

As this was my first child, I would be in hospital for a week, and that suited me fine since I knew that the baby and I would be well looked after. I would get all my meals for a change and a lot of rest, which I would need to help me cope with the baby when I finally took her home. It was great to have Margaret and the other women for company. They were a fantastic group, and we had some good laughs.

At about ten that evening, I was dozing off when a commotion outside the ward disturbed us all. Some men were arguing with a nurse who was telling them they were too late to visit. Suddenly, I recognised George's drunken, slurring voice and felt so embarrassed that I pretended to be asleep. I hoped the nurse was strong enough not to let him in. All the other women were sitting in their beds, wondering what was happening.

"Who on earth is that? They sound like drunks," Margaret whispered to me, and I stopped my pretence of sleeping.

"Yeah, they do," I said, trying not to show I knew exactly who it was.

There was more shouting, and suddenly, the door burst open, and we could hear the nurse saying, "Just five minutes then. Your wife and these other ladies need their rest."

As George and Brian, his best friend, staggered towards me I could scarcely believe they'd turned up in such a state. They looked as though they hadn't washed, shaved, or had a change of clothes for weeks. Both were swaying about and struggling to stay on their feet, and as for their speech, that could only possibly have been understood by someone who was also totally inebriated.

I sat on my bed and watched with horror as they made fools of themselves in front of the whole ward. George was leaning over the cot, breathing whiskey all over our baby daughter and making the most stupid noises I'd ever heard when talking to the baby. Luckily, she didn't wake, or her father would certainly have frightened her.

Two women at the other end of the ward thought George and his friend were funny and started laughing. Some of the others had joined in the laughter, not understanding what living with somebody like George was like. However, their laughter did ease the tension in the ward. It would have been much worse had they stuck their noses up at me because of them. When the nurse returned and told them it was time to leave, they acted as though she couldn't possibly be talking to them. They had an audience now, so they were going nowhere for the moment.

The nurse rang for assistance, and when two more nurses arrived, they had to throw George and his friend out. The ward soon calmed down, and we all settled down for the night. George didn't visit me again at the hospital, much to my relief. His first visit had been memorable enough to last me a lifetime. Margaret's visitors, very thoughtfully, did their best to make up for his absence.

Meanwhile, I was enjoying every moment I had with my precious baby girl. She was doing well, and I was slowly getting my strength back. All the other women seemed delighted when it was time to leave with their babies, but I was in no hurry to abandon the security of the hospital.

When one of the nurses asked what I would name her, I immediately replied, "Karen Michelle." I couldn't think why, as it wasn't a name I had even considered. It just came out of my mouth from nowhere, but she suited it. The day before I was due to leave, George's mother and aunt, Sheila, turned up at visiting time. My heart raced when I saw them approach my bed. I was in shock and didn't know how to act in front of them. What was she doing here? I didn't want that horrible woman anywhere near my child.

Sheila said my baby was beautiful and asked if I was doing okay. She was a much nicer person than her sister. It was hard to believe they were related, like chalk and cheese. I smiled at her and said I was fine, and she handed me a small present and a card for the baby. I opened it to find a gorgeous pink frilly dress and a matching cardigan. I was thanking her when Mrs McAteer shoved a bag into my hand; I squirmed.

"We can put our differences aside for George and his baby's sake," she said. "I won't say I've forgotten about your behaviour. After me taking ye in and all I did for ye. Still, I've decided to give ye a second chance."

I couldn't believe she had the nerve to speak to me this way. I could feel my temper rising and feared what I might say. Instead, I opened the bag, and there was a little blue dress with matching knickers. They were nice but couldn't compare to the quality of Sheila's gift.

"Thanks," was all I could muster.

I told her that I was going home the next day and would need George to bring the baby and me a set of clothes. She said she would pass on the message. I was relieved when visiting time was over and annoyed that she had intruded back into my life again. She even had the cheek to not acknowledge Karen as my daughter. It wasn't long ago that she was doing all she could to persuade George that the baby probably wasn't his.

I didn't want to let her get to me, but somehow, she had succeeded in sucking some of the joy out of my child's birth. In that brief visit, she had gotten to me, and once again, I felt inadequate. Somehow, I needed to stop this bitter woman from having any influence over my child.

The following day, Margaret and I were both going home with our new babies. She was ready early that morning, as her husband had brought in her and their baby's clothes the day before. When he came to pick her up, she looked lovely. She passed me a sheet of paper with her address and asked me to keep in touch. I waved her off and sat on my bed, hoping George would turn up soon with our clothes.

By lunchtime, I began to panic. I didn't even have the money to get a taxi, and I was starting to feel very embarrassed, especially when the nurses kept asking if there was any sign of my husband yet. I'd just about given up on him when he wandered in around four o'clock. He wasn't drunk, but I could tell he'd been in the pub. Fortunately, I was lucky to have my figure back quickly and fitted nicely into my old jeans and tee shirt. It felt fantastic not having my bump to carry around, and after my break in the hospital, I had a lot more energy.

George looked at Karen as though he were seeing her for the first time; he probably thought he was. "Oh well, we didn't get a boy then. Better luck next time," he quipped. I felt upset that he wasn't pleased about having a daughter, but I didn't dare say anything.

We had scarcely returned home for ten minutes when George was out the door again. "Well, I'm off to wet the wee baby's head," he said. What he meant was he was off to the pub to scrounge as many drinks as he could for the birth of our daughter.

Although a small part of me was disappointed that he hadn't taken more interest in his daughter, my overwhelming feeling was relief. I didn't want him hovering around me, making sly comments and demanding my time when all I wanted to focus on was Karen. I tried to rid my mind of any concerns I had about the drunken state he might be in when he returned and sat, staring at my beautiful daughter.

Karen lay in the middle of the bed, looking so tiny and helpless. I still found it hard to believe I had this beautiful child. She was like a little miracle that had come into my life. I sat with a mug of tea and looked at her, sleeping peacefully on the bed. When she woke, I would take her downstairs and show her off to Paddy. About an hour later, I picked her up and told her this was her home. Then, I sat on the bed, breastfed her, changed her nappy and put on the lovely outfit Sheila had bought for her.

Paddy was delighted to see the baby and slipped a half-crown into Karen's tiny hand for luck. "I've noticed that your husband doesn't hang around to help ye much. He needs to get his act together, or he could end up losing both of ye."

I appreciated him telling me what he thought rather than talking behind my back, and I knew he meant well.

"He likes the drink a bit too much," I replied awkwardly.

Just then, there was a knock on the door. It was Emma, smiling broadly as she stared at Karen in my arms. "I'm sorry I didn't get to see ye in the hospital, Frances, but I thought George and his family would be about. I heard ye were getting home today, so I'm here now." I was delighted to see her, and we headed up to the bedsit so I could introduce her properly to Karen and catch up on all the news.

"Well, you look great, and she's gorgeous. What have ye called her?

I placed Karen into her arms and said, "Karen Michelle, this is Emma, and she's going to be your godmother." For a moment, I thought Emma would cry as she gazed down at Karen, watching every expression on her little face. It was a lovely, emotional moment watching Emma holding Karen. I knew I had picked the right person to be my daughter's godmother.

I opened the presents from Emma and her mother. There was a cute teddy bear and a wee fluffy rabbit. I told her they were great, and I hadn't got any toys for her yet. I knew that Karen would love them when she got a bit older.

We talked about how I had felt when Mrs McAteer turned up at the hospital, and then I told her all about George and Brian being drunk when they came to visit. Emma was annoyed and said that it must have been humiliating for me.

Later, I made another cup of tea while she went to the chippy and got us some sausages and chips and some fizzy drinks. We talked late into the night until Emma had to get a taxi home. George still hadn't returned home, so I went to bed.

At about three o'clock the following afternoon, George's brother, John, brought him home. "He's been wetting the baby's head,'" he said, laughing at the state George was in.

George collapsed on the bed and was out cold. John stopped for a while to see the baby and said she was the image of me. I felt pleased about that and hoped he was right. With how I felt about George and Mrs McAteer, Karen resembling either of them would have annoyed me. I imagine that anyone in my shoes would have felt the same way.

Over the next few months, I tried to be the best mother I could be to my beautiful daughter. I loved every moment I spent with her. When she was awake, I would shower her with hugs and kisses and talk or sing to her constantly as though she could understand everything I was saying. She was the most essential thing in my life and, most of the time, my only company.

Emma came to see us whenever she could, but she was preparing to go to Belfast University. I was pleased for her, but I knew how much I would miss her. She would have a new life there, with a new set of friends. I worried that she might forget all about me and

Karen. She promised that she would never fail us, which she never did. She promised to visit soon.

Mrs McConnell had been to see us several times and had brought a lot of baby clothes. I was enormously grateful to her for them. When I took my baby out and about, I felt proud that she was dressed as well as anybody else's baby. I loved it when people stopped in the street to admire her.

Mrs McAteer had ordered George, and he ordered me, to bring the baby to see her, which I had done several times, just to keep the peace. Things still felt very strained with her, but it was great to see Max again. He looked like a proud grandad as he held Karen in his arms.

Unfortunately, even with his new daughter, George remained unchanged. He was out drinking as much as ever and I only seemed to see him when he was plastered and needed my help getting into bed. With Karen to care for, I was getting very little sleep and was beginning to feel drained. I had started taking a nap during the day, whenever Karen was sleeping, but I hadn't slept properly since leaving the hospital.

One morning, at around seven thirty, I woke to the sound of Karen crying. Exhausted, I could barely keep my eyes open as I struggled to drag myself out of bed. I had been up at two o'clock in the morning with her and then again with George, who had been delivered home, drunk, at about four in the morning. Unfortunately, on this occasion, instead of crashing straight out, he started singing Elvis songs at the top of his voice. The racket had woken Karen again, and I hadn't gotten back to sleep until after six o-clock.

I fed and changed Karen again, then sat rocking her in my arms to keep her quiet. George would not have been happy if she had woken him up. The last time she'd woken him, he'd started screaming at me, "Can't you shut her up? What sort of mother are ye anyway!" That was George on a good day. On a bad day, he might wreck the flat, punch me, or both. So, I had to make sure she didn't cry.

By the time George surfaced, Karen had been asleep for a few hours. He told me to make him fried eggs on toast before he headed up the road to his mother's house. When he had left, shortly after finishing his breakfast, I breathed a sigh of relief, climbed back into bed and closed my eyes.

Suddenly, I was widely awakened by the strong smell of something burning and saw the frying pan was on fire. I reacted quickly, jumping out of bed and pouring the water from the kettle over it, but rather than putting it out the flames got more extensive and the curtains caught on fire. Panic-stricken, my only thought was to grab Karen and get out as fast as possible.

I ran down to the bottom of the stairs with Karen, but I wasn't sure what to do next. I didn't want to tell Paddy because I knew he would be upset. Then I remembered that Paddy had moved someone into one of the rooms on the first floor. I knocked on the door, and a man in his late twenties answered, wearing only his jeans. I told him I lived at the top and that my room was on fire.

"Wait there!" he said, dashing past me. Moments later, he came running down with a tea towel wrapped around his hand and holding the pan, still in flames. He dashed past, warning me to stay back, and continued down the stairs and out the back door. Leaving the burning pan in the backyard, he hurried back upstairs to ensure the rest of the fire was out.

"It's okay now: the fire is out, but you won't be able to take your baby up there for a while. There's some smoke damage, and the smell is awful. I have opened your window. Do ye want to come in? I'll make ye a wee cup of tea. You've had a bit of a shock."

He introduced himself as David, "Well, this is one way of meeting the neighbours, but ye just should have knocked and said hello."

"I'm Frances," I replied, gratefully.

Later that day, I ventured up to my little bedsit to assess the extent of the damage. The sight of it was disheartening, and it was clear that returning to this space with a newborn was out of the question. The once-cosy sanctuary I had painstakingly prepared for my baby's arrival now lay in ruins, leaving me feeling utterly lost and hopeless. Despite the overwhelming uncertainty that loomed over me, one thing remained steadfastly clear in my mind. There would be no question of me and Karen moving back in with George's mother. I couldn't subject myself and my child to the toxicity of Mrs McAteer's house, no matter what George might say, to try to convince me. It was a resolve born out of necessity, a determination to protect myself and my unborn child from further harm, no matter the cost.

A Bomb in the Army Camp

After the fire, we moved into a house across the road from George's family. It was the last thing I wanted, but George thought it was perfect as he would be able to pop across to his mother anytime. The house owner, Paul, was a single man in his late sixties. He was out most of the day, only using the house to sleep in at night. The arrangement would have worked well if it had been anywhere else, but as it was across the road from George's mother's house, Mrs McAteer felt that she could come over to interfere or complain whenever she felt like it.

I planned to always keep the doors locked and to pretend not to be in whenever I saw her coming. However, the plan didn't always work as she would watch out for any visitors coming to my door and then catch me out when I opened it.

It quickly became a nightmare for me. Mrs McAteer was soon spread her vile rumours and malicious gossip to anyone who would listen; causing even more friction between George and me. It was in her nature to stir things up. On one occasion, after she had been whispering poison in George's ear, he returned home drunk at two thirty in the morning, grabbed the mattress, hurling me out of bed and across the floor. I woke up as he began screaming at me. I couldn't understand what he was saying, except that his mother had told him something. What that could have been, as I spent most of my time at home looking after Karen, I had no idea.

When the noise woke Karen up, I left George to his rantings and spent the night with her in her little bed. George must have been too drunk to move as he fell asleep on the floor. In the morning, he had forgotten what had happened, and I wasn't going to be the one to remind him.

Not long after moving in, when Karen was only a few months old, I discovered I was pregnant again. The pregnancy was unplanned and would have been the result of one of George's drunken encounters. In those moments, his complete disregard for me was painfully evident: sometimes he would penetrate me even while I slept, thinking only of his own self-gratification and the power he enjoyed exercising over me.

In Northern Ireland at that time, it seemed that Catholic men were given free rein over their wives' bodies to do whatever the hell they wanted. George loved it when the priest exalted the virtues of female obedience. Men like George could pretty much get away with anything while women had no rights, and no one wanted to hear you whining about it. So just like the expression, "It is what it is," that's what it was.

Life was hard, and I was about to bring another child into the world. The troubles were worsening daily, and people rarely talked about anything else. It was depressing as, on top of all the everyday problems we had to cope with, there was the constant worry that you or your family might be the next to get blown up or shot. Many of those injured were completely innocent and it all seemed so pointless; I wished desperately for it all to end.

The impact of the troubles on my everyday life was taking its toll. Whenever there was a bombing on the news my anxiety levels would spike, triggering a heightened sense of vigilance. Every passing car, especially Ford Cortinas, sent a shiver of apprehension down my spine - these vehicles were often used by the police as unmarked cars. Similarly, the sight of a parked white van would fill me with dread since they were frequently used by the IRA as vessels for much larger bombs. The fear of them blowing up, as I pushed the pram past them, was with me constantly; and shootings were now a daily occurrence.

Living under the constant shadow of fear, the oppressive presence of constant surveillance and the inconvenience of having your bags and the pram searched whenever you entered a shop had somehow become part of our everyday life. Still, life had to go on: people went about their business, what else they could do, they still had to work, shop and look after their children.

As the months passed and pregnancy progressed my concerns for my daughter continued to grow and I knew I would be doubly worried once the new baby arrived. The morning sickness was as bad as before, but I was more knowledgeable and better prepared this time around and so better able to cope with it.

I thought that it would be good for Karen to have the company of a little brother or sister and I was already talking to her about it.

With Karen as my only companion, I devoted much of my time to her. She was a bright wee thing and watching her pull herself up on the furniture to taking her tentative first steps, filled me with pride. I spent a lot of time talking to her and she was already starting to say some words clearly, she was quick to pick them up. I went about my day singing and she would try to sing along with me.

On the 8th August 1973, when Karen was only eleven months old, I gave birth to my second daughter. She was beautiful, just like her sister, and we named her Deborah, after George's oldest sister. The name was not my choice, although I did like it. However, I would have preferred it if George had asked me first.

I stayed in the hospital for twenty-four hours because it was a second birth. I was relieved when the doctor did his rounds and said I could go home. I hadn't made any friends in the hospital. I had become bored of lying about reading the same magazines over and over.

I remembered to bring the baby's clothes along with my own to the hospital this time. I had learnt not to count on George for anything. I had put some money away for a cab home. I was ready to go and felt excited, wondering what Karen would make of her little sister. I gazed at Deborah, thinking how lucky I was to have two beautiful daughters.

As I waited on the bed for the cab to arrive, I could hear the nurses talking about a bomb that had gone off in the Army camp in Omagh, which was very close to where we lived. I hadn't heard about it until now, but it had happened the previous day. One of the nurses said that three pregnant women and some children were among the sixteen who had been injured; miraculously, no one had been killed. The bomb was in a hijacked post office van, and it was packed with 350lb of explosives. Driven into the army-camp, it exploded near the married-quarters causing extensive damage to dozens of houses and blowing the roof off many more.

Back home, everyone who visited was talking about the aftermath of yet another bombing: this time much closer to home. There was a notable sense of panic around the town as people tried to carry on with their lives. The spectre of violence loomed large, casting a shadow of fear over our community as we struggled to carry on with our daily lives amidst the chaos.

Once again, I found myself praying to the universe for a solution to the Troubles. I longed for peace, to bring my children up safely without fear and without worrying about what religion they, and those around them, were. It seemed now as though there were always bombs going off or riots happening somewhere in Ulster. This one reminded me of how close they could get, and I worried for my daughters. It wasn't a good time to welcome a new child.

Although Karen was only eleven months old, she was walking and talking very well, and people often found it hard to believe how young she was. She loved having a baby sister and was very protective of her. Karen tried climbing into the cot with Deborah. She could not understand why Deborah could not get up and play with her. Not even the sound of Deborah's constant crying seemed to put Karen off wanting to be with her little sister. I was surprised that she was not jealous of all the attention that Deborah demanded from me. There was little time left for everything we used to do together.

Deborah was a beautiful baby, and I loved her from the moment she was born. I had not expected her to be any different from when I was raising Karen. So, it was a shock to find there was nothing I could do to settle her. She cried night and day, a horrible screeching sound, and she appeared to be in constant pain. Sometimes, she would get into such a state that she would stop breathing altogether. It was terrifying!

As the months wore on, and the crying continued, I became so exhausted and run down that I worried about how I was going to carry on. There appeared to be nothing I could do to comfort Deborah. The health visitor and doctor could find no reason why she would not settle. They told me I was doing everything right and to persevere with it. However, she just would not stop!

There were times when I felt so desperate and depressed, and I'm ashamed to admit this, that I even contemplated suicide. Then later, when Karen was tucked up in bed, I would feel guilty for thinking that I could even consider putting my children through that nightmare, especially as I knew only too well how abandonment felt, especially for a small child.

On one of my visits to Doctor McMullan, he told me that I was suffering from postnatal depression. He said I could work through it only with my husband's support and practical help. I appreciated his concern for me as my doctor and as someone I considered a friend. He had put himself out of his way to protect me and find me work in a decent home. Although I knew George would never entertain any request for help and support, I was so desperately trying to hold on to my sanity that I told him what Doctor McMullan had advised. I really shouldn't have bothered!

"Ye, it's not depression, Frances, it's all in your head." was his response. "What do ye have to be depressed about? My mother coped with all of us and never got depressed. In the future, ye won't talk about our own fucking business to anybody. Do ye hear me!" he screamed, then stormed out, leaving me feeling even more alone and inadequate.

I collapsed onto a nearby chair, sobbing uncontrollably, knowing I would never ask for his help again. It was infuriating, having to cope on my own while having to listen to all the lies about how his mother coped better than any other human being. That woman spent her life taking credit for other people's good deeds. The family would never disagree with her, while the neighbours would only do so behind her back.

Mrs McAteer would have brought up her children with assistance from Max and other family members. She would never have let them get away with not helping.

Over the coming weeks, I tried my hardest to cope better. I dared not let Deborah disturb George or Mr Gileese. Walking up and down the house with her each night, I tried to convince myself that I didn't need to sleep. However, it wasn't long before it took its toll on me and, one morning, I collapsed outside the local shop. Fortunately, a neighbour brought me home and called the doctor, who told me I was suffering from exhaustion and was dangerously rundown.

"I'm admitting your baby to the hospital for a few weeks to undergo some tests," the doctor said. "Even if we can't find the reason for her crying, at least you will get some well-earned rest."

I felt like a failure as a mother and dreaded George's family finding out. George paid no attention to Deborah, and it had cross my mind that this could be part of the problem. I thought that babies could sense these things; that they needed love from both of us. His disappointment at her not being a boy was clear to see and heartbreaking. How must that have felt for Deborah, I wondered?

I walked along the road with Karen to the hospital every day to see her little sister. We would stop at the shop for a few sweets and a comic. We stayed until the nurses forced me to go home and get some sleep. She was in a side ward, and the nurses who ran tests on her were welcoming and doing a great job looking after her. However, they couldn't find anything wrong with Deborah, which was a relief. They thought she just had a good pair of lungs and one day, hopefully, she would stop crying. They wanted to keep her in a little longer as they were concerned that I needed more time to recover. I was immensely grateful for that, and it was a huge relief to get a decent night's sleep at the end of the day. At least, that is, until George staggered home drunk. But, once he crashed out, I was then able to sleep through until morning.

Karen was delighted to have more of my attention again now that her sister was hospitalised. Our mornings were filled with her laughter and singing her favourite songs. It was wonderful to hear her being happy. Whenever I could manage it, I would get us out of the house before George woke up and spoilt things.

When I picked Deborah up from the hospital, she was still crying, and as the nurse passed by, she looked at me with an expression of pity on her face. Although they had been unable to find anything wrong with Deborah, I couldn't help but wonder if they had missed something.

I felt more rested now with more energy and able to give Deborah my full attention. I knew that Karen would help, as much as she could, and we were both happy to bring her home. I planned to get the girls out of the house as much as possible: going to the park and for long walks with the pram. Hopefully this would be a distraction for Deborah and would ease her crying. It was time for a change, and I wasn't going to be stuck at home all day just in case George decided to pop in for something to eat.

Karen loved that idea and early the next morning she was up and ready to go out straight after some breakfast. We fed Deborah her bottle and rusks and placed her in her pram. She cried, but I grabbed the bag I had prepared with nappies, juice, bottles and a few changes of clothes and we left the house - with George still in bed - heading out into the fresh morning air. Deborah cried for a little while longer but fell asleep eventually with the rocking of the pram. I felt at peace and was happy that it all felt right for the moment.

A Home of Our Own

Finally, we had been allocated a brand-new council house, our first real home. I hoped the move to a new house, away from all the interference of Mrs McAteer and others, would help settle Deborah. I had grown tired of all the advice and old remedies recommended to me by everyone, none of which worked. I put my daughters in the pram, and, full of excitement, I went to the council housing office to pick up the keys. The man in the council office told me to wait at least six months before I did any decorating. He explained that the plaster wouldn't have dried out yet. I could paint or paper when the plaster was completely dry. I thanked him and made my way to the new housing estate.

Workers were still on the site, and I struggled with the pram as I tried to push it over the rubble. Somehow, I found the right house and put the key in the door. It opened with no trouble, and I was immediately overwhelmed: being in a brand-new house, with everything untouched and perfect, felt fantastic. I was so grateful to have my own home. It smelled strongly of plaster, wood, and putty, and I loved its spaciousness.

There was a large kitchen-diner with good cupboard space and a brand-new cooker. The living room was spacious, with a large window on one wall and a modern fireplace in the centre of another. Upstairs were two good-sized bedrooms, a bathroom, and a large airing cupboard. There was a small garden out front and a larger one at the back that looked out onto woodland. Some of the woodland had been cut back to build the council estate.

As I wandered around, it would hardly sink in that I would live here. I knew it would take a while before I could make it a proper home - filling it with furniture, carpet, and curtains - but it was mine, and I was on cloud nine!

Karen ran around the house exploring. She loved the tapping sound her shoes made on the floorboards. I swayed Deborah back and forth in my arms to keep her from crying and watched Karen, who was laughing as she banged her feet down hard and listened as the sound echoed through the empty house. It was a delight to see her so happy.

George had told me to go ahead as Brian would give him a lift later with our few pieces of furniture in the van. I had nothing to do now but entertain the children until they arrived. I hoped that the new house would put George in a good mood. The time passed very slowly, and when they came, about five hours later, I was sitting on the hard living room floor singing songs to amuse my daughters.

George and Brian, and one of our new neighbours, carried the furniture and boxes in. I soon searched the pots and pans and began making dinner: potatoes, sausages, peas and gravy. Deborah was propped up with a pillow in her pram so that she could see me, but she still cried. When Brian saw me struggling, he picked her up so I could finish the meal. George wasn't good around crying babies, even his own, and he certainly didn't see it as his job to comfort her or help me.

Brian stayed for dinner and seemed to enjoy every bit of it. When I cleared the dishes away and started washing them, I heard him telling George to look after me.

"Ye don't want to lose that wee woman, George," he insisted. "She's priceless, like a wee pot of gold."

George didn't answer and appeared annoyed that I was getting a compliment from his friend. George didn't do compliments and saw anything I did as nothing more than a wife's duty. "Come on now, Brian, we need to be going," he insisted, grabbing his coat. Brian got to his feet and rubbed his belly.

"Thanks for the food, Frances. Yeah did a grand job."

As the months passed, I worked hard to turn the house into a home for my children. I wanted them to have the sort of home that I'd never had, and finally, it was beginning to take shape. Shortly after we moved in, Mrs McConnell delivered all the furniture from my old bedroom at her house. She said she'd like me to have it, and she also told me that she hadn't let anyone stay in my room since I'd left. Her kindness and generosity never ceased to amaze me. I couldn't understand why she would bother to help me. I knew that nothing in her house would be cheap, and I carefully polished the wooden pieces daily.

Other people had also been kind enough to give us bits and pieces. When George's grandparents died, and their furniture was divided up, he acquired a vast, wooden dining table and six chairs - with red velvet on the seats and edged with brass studs. George said his grandparents had had them for as long as he could remember, and they would be worth quite a bit if he ever sold them. They fitted nicely onto the dining area of the kitchen.

By now, I'd given up all hope that things could ever get better between George and me. In the privacy of our new house, his true colours showed through, and the abuse worsened. It was no longer just a slap or a punch I'd receive when he was in a bad mood. I could scarcely believe it one evening when he announced that he was going to give me a good kicking, as he liked to call it. Then, when he returned home drunk, he proceeded to do so.

It was in the early hours of the morning when he staggered in. I answered the door because he had forgotten his keys. George complained that I'd taken my time getting out of bed to answer the door. By the time he'd finished with me, I was left black and blue, with bruises on my back, legs, and around my ribs. I had a black eye that was swollen, and I couldn't open it properly. Afterwards, he warned me not to tell anyone what he'd done or let anyone see the bruises, threatening to take a knife to me if I did.

I had become terrified of George, especially when he drank, and believed he could do anything to me. It was a relief that the children hadn't woken up that night to see him attacking me. Karen constantly asked what was wrong with my eye and tried to kiss it better. I told her that I was silly and walked into the door.

I kept myself shut in, only going to the shop when I had to and at quiet times of the day, keeping my head down and not stopping to talk to anyone. I hid if anyone came to the door, pretending I wasn't in. It went on for weeks until the bruising had vanished. Over the following months, the kickings became more regular. Somehow, they had become my way of life!

One night, when Deborah was eight months old, I put her in her cot, as usual, and waited outside the door. I always left her crying for a while to see if she'd drop off to sleep and only picked her up when I thought she would do some damage, like stop breathing. I always ended up having to go back in and get her. Her face would be red and soaked from her tears.

I paused there, waiting for her to start screaming, but there wasn't a sound. I waited a while longer, and she was still quiet. After five more minutes, I crept down each stair and into the living room, where Karen watched television, and I sat beside her. It felt odd to sit down with Karen, and I realised how accustomed I had grown to the sound of Deborah crying.

After ten minutes, I started to wonder if she was all right. Then panic set in. I had a horrible thought that she might be dead, and I ran up to check that she was still breathing. She lay there, still in her cot, and I crept towards her, looking for a sign that she was still alive. As I stroked her tiny hand, her fingers moved. I felt relieved but also ridiculous for imagining that she was dead. It was just such a shock that she'd settled down like that. The following day, she woke up in a lovely mood, and I never had a problem with her again. It was as if I had a different child. Whatever it was that had made her cry would remain a mystery.

Karen began taking a lot more interest in her little sister. She became overly protective of her now rather than running off to avoid the screaming. It was amazing to watch her singing to Deborah as if to teach her every word of the song. Deborah, however, was not interested in learning to sing, but that didn't deter Karen from trying. Deborah was only interested in food and watching television.

As she got older, she mostly enjoyed digging in the dirt in our back garden, unlike her sister, who had to have everything clean. They were my joy! It was such a pity that George was always ready to spoil it. Why, I wished, couldn't he stay living with his mother who deserved him?

A Welcome Visitor

One morning, I answered a knock at the door to discover a gipsy woman offering clothes pegs for sale. Mindful of the superstition that it's unlucky to turn away a gipsy empty-handed, I purchased a few. As she handed me the pegs, her gaze bore into mine for a moment before she spoke, "Thank ye, Mrs, take care of yourself and your wee children, especially the one you're carrying now. I can see ye with a wee son in your arms before too long." With those words, she turned and knocked on the neighbour's door.

I wasn't aware I was pregnant, but I believed the gipsy. Something about her manner told me she wasn't just guessing. Also, she had come to my door to sell pegs, not to tell my fortune. I'd have had to cross her palm with silver first for that. I couldn't get her words out of my mind. As soon as I'd fallen pregnant with each of the girls, I felt nauseous. However, I didn't feel anything to suggest I was pregnant now.

I took the girls out for fresh air and called in at the doctor's surgery. I told the receptionist I needed a pregnancy test, and she sent me to the treatment room. Afterwards, the nurse told me to make an appointment with my doctor to get the results. I was glad I'd done the test and thought I could put it out of my mind until I got the results.

Deborah had fallen asleep in the pram. Walking along the road in the sunshine was peaceful. Karen stopped regularly to pick daisies, handing them to me to make a daisy chain. I gathered them in the pram until we came to the park. I decided not to go straight home and stopped to let Karen run around and play. She always loved it when we stopped at the park.

She sat on the grass and watched while I threaded the daisies to make a necklace for her. She tried to help, but the daisies kept breaking, so she gave up and spun around to make her dress float out. Deborah preferred to sit and watch and didn't like being spun around. However, she did always find it amusing watching her sister. All the spinning made Karren dizzy, and she fell onto the grass, laughing at how silly she looked.

"Hello, it's Frances, isn't it? I'm Nula; I live next door to ye." I'd seen her from my kitchen window but was too embarrassed to speak to her. I was sure she must have heard George yelling at me. She was an attractive girl around my age but much taller with a slim figure and shoulder-length light brown hair. Like me, she usually wore jeans and a sweatshirt. I had stopped wearing skirts and dresses since coming out of the convent. Maybe I was rebelling because I would never have been allowed to wear jeans growing up with the nuns. They were considered too tomboyish.

Nula had a pushchair with her son, Sean, in it. He was around one and a half years old, around the same age as Karen. He seemed to be a happy child and kept smiling at me.

"Yeah, I'm Frances. It's nice to meet ye, Nula," I answered, getting myself up off the grass. I felt awful for not speaking to her before now. She must have thought I was a bit strange or snobby for not being more friendly. I would have spoken, but I often hid the bruises that George had inflicted upon me. I also knew that George wouldn't like it if I talked to the neighbours. He would immediately assume that I was telling them all about his abusive behaviour.

She lifted Sean from his pushchair, and he and Karen toddled off happily together. "They are playing well together, Frances. Will ye come round for a coffee when we get back home? I don't know about you, but I get fed up with the house all day with no one to talk to."

I felt worried about being at her house when George got home, but then I got annoyed with myself for letting George dictate every moment of my life. I should be able to speak to people if I wanted to. He probably wouldn't be home for ages, not until he was well and truly drunk.

"Yeah, I'd love to come round," I replied, feeling very rebellious and somewhat brave. I realised then just how boring my life had become with every minute spent around the children worrying about what George would do next. It felt unfair that he could do whatever he wanted, without question, while I had to do as he said.

On the way home, Nula told me that her husband was English and had just left the Army. She said this was the reason why they didn't know many people. They were worried about the IRA finding out and shooting him. I could understand her concerns: the Troubles were getting worse, with bombings and shootings a daily occurrence, and people had to be careful about who they spoke to. I was delighted that she trusted me enough to confide in me. I liked her and thought we could be great friends.

Later, we sat in Nula's kitchen, drinking coffee while Karen and Sean played in the back garden. When she asked what my husband did for a living, I told her that he had just started doing a milk run with his friend Brian. "They go round the farms, collecting the milk and delivering it to Nestle's factory. Brian drives the lorry while George helps to load the churns," I explained. "Then, when they finish, at about two o'clock, they're off to the pub."

She gave me a sympathetic look, and I felt that she wanted to say something but was holding back. I didn't want to drag her into my misery and to be involved with mine and George's troubles. I was afraid that it might change her mind about being my friend.

Just then, Deborah began to cry, and I needed to take her home for a nappy change and a feed. Nula suggested I leave Karen there and come back when I was done. She offered to make some dinner for the kids. By the time I'd returned, Nula had made the kids fish fingers, chips, and beans. She looked happy to have found a little friend for Sean and seemed in no hurry for us to leave, so I sat down and enjoyed another coffee and a good long chat.

When I returned home, it was time to prepare the girls for bed. Karen was so happy to have Sean as her friend and kept asking if she could play with him tomorrow. I told her he would have to be a special secret friend between me and her. I explained that not even her daddy could know because if people found out, she might be stopped from seeing him. She agreed and appeared to understand what I was saying.

That evening, I sat and thought about my exciting day. It felt great to have a friend again. I hadn't had a good chat with anyone since Emma had left for university. I'd missed her and our talks, and I hoped she would come and visit me soon. We didn't even send letters for fear George would find them. His paranoia had become worse since he had started drinking more. She would not be happy with how everything was working out with George, but she knew better than anyone who he was when he was drunk.

Over the next few weeks, I spent much of the time at Nula's house while George was out. It was easy keeping it a secret from him as he was never home during the day. However, I had yet to invite Nula to come to my house in case he would return unexpectedly. She didn't seem to mind, but I felt I owed her an explanation. I wanted to tell her what it was like for me living with George and that I wasn't being rude, but it was hard to know where to begin.

We walked to the doctor one morning, and my pregnancy was confirmed. "Congratulations, Frances. I bet George will be pleased," Nula said, obviously delighted for me.

"Yeah, but only if it's a boy," I blurted out without thinking.

"Well, he probably would want a son after two daughters. Still, he'd be happy even if it was another girl," she said.

I looked away and didn't answer, afraid she might see my mask slip and see how I felt about George. I'd met her husband, Mark, who was very friendly and, unlike me and George, Nula looked genuinely happy around him.

We left the surgery and strolled to the park. We were sitting, watching our children play, when Nula told me I could trust her if I needed to talk about anything. She said she would be there for me. It was my chance to get everything out in the open. I began by telling her that George had always wanted a boy and was disappointed I'd had girls.

"Is that why he's always down the pub?" she inquired.

"God, no. He was getting drunk long before I had the girls, but it has become much worse."

"Frances, I don't mean to be out of order, and ye can tell me to mind my own business if ye want to, but we know about George beating ye up when he gets drunk. We can hear him through the walls and hear ye crying and pleading with him to stop. Mark was about to go round the other night and sort him out, but I said that we might make things worse for ye."

It was such a relief to me that she knew: now I didn't have to explain, but I was embarrassed that they'd heard him.

"We've known for ages, but I didn't know ye well enough to say anything. I was hoping ye could tell me yourself, as I didn't want to offend ye," she assured me. Tears of relief flowed down my cheeks, and Nula put an arm around my shoulders.

"If ye ever need help, just give us a big bang on the wall."

Back at her house, we talked for hours about George and his mother. Then I told her about my life in the convent. She listened with a great deal of interest and compassion.

"So ye don't have anyone you can go to if ye wanted to leave him," she said.

"No, Nula, I don't. It looks like I'm stuck with him for life. If I did have family, who gave a damn, I wouldn't be with him now. I think sometimes that if I did have a family, he wouldn't have the guts to carry on like that."

It felt liberating to get everything out to her. Usually, our conversations revolved around our children. This seemed like our first proper conversation since discussing her concerns for her husband. At least now I could be straight with her, and she'd understand why I couldn't invite her to my house.

It wasn't until I'd put the girls to bed that I had time to think about the child I would have. The gipsy woman had been right about my pregnancy, and I felt confident that she was also right about it being a boy. I wondered how it would affect George and me: whether it would change him in any way. He hadn't noticed the girls much: he saw it as my job to deal with them. I wondered if a son would be any different. Would he want to be out there playing football and going fishing with him?

He'd often said that having a boy would prove he was a man. I never understood that, and he repeatedly blamed me for being unable to produce a son for him. He would often accuse me of being useless and tell me there was something wrong with me. At least that was something he wouldn't be able to bring up to me again.

The following day, Karen came in and jumped on my bed. There was no sound from Deborah yet, so I took her in beside me for a big hug. The sun beamed through the gap in the curtains, and I took a moment to focus my eyes. I learned, then, that George hadn't come home during the night which wasn't particularly unusual. He had stayed away for days before, on a binge of drinking and whatever else he got up to. I did concern myself with what he was doing, or maybe I just didn't care.

I was glad he'd stayed out because I'd woken up feeling rested. Not having him there was good for us and we were better for it. I knew it wouldn't last because sooner or later, he would be home, and everything would change. It was not the first time I wished he'd never come home again: our lives would be much better without him.

Karen played "Round and Round the Garden" on my hand and tried tickling me. When I played it back and began tickling her, she laughed so much she woke her sister. I lifted Deborah from her cot and went to the kitchen to get the children their breakfast. I'd just sat down with a cup of tea when there was a knock at the door.

I went to answer it with Karen hanging on to my nighty and heard a voice calling, "Hello, Frances." I couldn't believe it when I opened the door and saw my sister Sinead. She looked beautiful, much taller than me now, with her long blond hair and big brown eyes. Wearing a new cream-coloured trouser suit. I assumed life was treating her well, and I felt dowdy next to her. My emotions were all over the place, and I burst into tears and hugged her tight. I'd not seen her since my wedding day and often wondered how she was doing.

"Karen and Debbie, this is your auntie," I shouted to the girls in the kitchen. Debbie had crawled under the kitchen table and didn't want to leave. Karen said, "Hello," and then went a bit shy, which was unusual since she'd usually talk to anyone. However, they soon came around when Sinead took two packets of biscuits from a carrier bag and gave them a couple each.

I took them into the living room, switched the television on to a children's programme, and then went to pour Sinead a cup of tea. She stopped me, saying she'd got something better, and produced a bottle of wine from her bag. She insisted I join her in a glass, and we sat down for a chat. She told me she'd been to Mrs McAteer's house and that one of George's brothers told her I had moved. She hadn't seen George and said she didn't think he was there.

I soon discovered she wasn't just visiting but needed somewhere to live. When she asked if she could stay with me for a while, I couldn't turn her away, but I knew I'd be in trouble when George found out. She could tell I was worried and asked how things were going. I told her I was expecting my third child and was unhappy with George. "He drinks away any money we get, Sinead, and I can hardly afford to feed the children or myself. He won't like it, but ye can stay; you're my sister."

"Does he hit ye, Frances, because if he does, I'll kill that bastard?" I could see the anger on her face, and I could understand it as we had both already suffered a lot of abuse growing up in the convent. The memory of that would stay with us forever.

"Yeah, he does, Sinead, but ye can't say anything, or you'll make things worse for me. Promise me ye won't say anything because he'll go mad if he knows I've told ye."

"Okay then, if that's the way ye want it. However, I won't promise that I will just stand and watch it if he hits you in front of me," she said.

We'd sat drinking wine and chatting about our childhood in the convent. As terrible as they were, those memories were all we had in common. I suppose when we tried to tell anyone else about them, they couldn't understand how horrific it had been. Sinead said she would never let anyone treat her like that ever again. Although she had never liked George very much, his abuse of me was why she hated him. She told me a little about where she'd been living and what she had been up to. We'd almost finished the bottle when the conversation returned to George again. Before I knew it, we were planning, how to kill him. It began in fun, but we both realised how better life would be for us all without him. We knew he wasn't ever going to let me leave him.

"If ye put rat poison in his food, Frances, it will do the job. It contains arsenic, and it can't be detected in the body," she suggested. Ye must get someone else to buy it though because you have to sign for it. I saw that on a programme on the telly about a month ago,"

I laughed loudly and suggested to her that she had watched too many murder films. Although we were both entirely serious, some of the ideas we came up with were ridiculous, and soon we were giggling.

"Wait till he's asleep and go up with the heaviest saucepan ye can find, then hit him as hard as ye can with it." This was only one of Sinead's crazy ideas.

"What if I don't hit him hard enough to kill him, and he gets up and kills me? Anyway, that's not self-defence: that's trying to kill someone when they're asleep, and I'd end up in jail!" Then the children would be without a mother.

That just made us laugh even more. I couldn't understand why we were finding this all so funny. Maybe it was partly the wine affecting us, but it was a release to imagine George dead. We were in hysterics when Karen walked in to ask for another biscuit. She began to laugh, too, because she wasn't used to seeing me laughing like this. Everything seemed funny to us, and I was so happy that Sinead came to stay.

Sinead asked me to walk with her to the bus depot to collect her bags. She'd asked the lost property man to look after them. I got the girls ready, got dressed, tidied myself up and headed into town with her.

George passed us in his friend's lorry and pulled over to the side of the road. "Where are ye off to?" he shouted.

I went over to explain that Sinead needed somewhere to stay and that I couldn't very well turn her away. He looked hung over and annoyed with me but tried not to show it in front of Brian. Throwing Sinead a filthy look, he said, "Yeh better sign on for work then because we're not keeping ye for nothing."

"Yeah, George, it's nice to see you too," she replied sarcastically.

I tried to break the tension by telling him I was going to have another baby. It seemed to do the trick as he smiled at Brian and said, "Maybe I'll get my son this time. Don't be too long because I need ye home to make me something to eat," he said. They drove off down the road, but I had a bad feeling that it wasn't the end of it. He didn't look pleased to see my sister. Sinead wasn't bothered by him, but she was concerned for me and couldn't believe the predicament I found myself in with George.

The Punch Bag

The next few months were much better for me. George hated Sinead and didn't care what she thought of him, but he didn't want anyone to see his abusive side. He stayed away from the house as much as possible and was much quieter when he came home. I felt safer but knew it wouldn't last and could sense the tension building in him. He wasn't used to not being himself.

One day, he came home with a punch bag and spent the morning working on suspending it from the middle of our bedroom ceiling. I was delighted because I thought that perhaps it would stop him from using me as one. A few days later, he got out all the posters and magazine cuttings about Bruce Lee, which he'd collected over the years, from a box in the wardrobe. He then began putting tape on them and covering the bedroom walls with them. I thought he was losing his mind, as he was obsessed about where he would place each one.

I was horrified when I saw the bedroom transformed into what could only be described as a shrine, but I kept my mouth shut. I knew I would just have to live with it. Sinead suggested that George had a screw loose and that I should be worried about what he might get up to next. I had to agree with her as it was hard to argue against it.

From then on, George would come home, use the punch bag and exercise for a few hours every day before going to the pub. He took it very seriously. The sound of him shouting, as he punched and kicked, echoed through the house, and we were all relieved when he eventually stopped and got ready to go out. Also, I was worried that the ceiling would cave in, and we might lose the house.

"Frances, what on earth's that noise coming from your house?" Nula asked on one of my visits next door.

I told her all about the punch bag and posters, "Apparently, he's going to have the mind and strength of Bruce Lee and the body of Charles Atlas," I said sarcastically, and we laughed at how ridiculous it sounded. I was sure that the people he wanted to be like didn't finish off their exercises by going to the pub, smoking continuously, and getting drunk.

"Well, if he's taking it all out on the punch bag, at least he's leaving you alone," she said.

A few weeks later, Sinead started getting money from the dole office and decided to return to Belfast for a week. She'd had a letter from her ex-boyfriend, Kieran, whom she hadn't got over and wanted to see him. I understood that she had to follow her heart. I obviously couldn't stop her, so I walked her to the bus station and was soon waving her off. I felt sick with nerves as I walked back to the house: dreading facing George without her there by my side.

When I returned, George was in the kitchen boiling a pan of soya beans for protein. He poured some of the water into a mug and began drinking it. I thought, from the expressions on his face, that it must have tasted as disgusting as it smelled.

"I have to drink a lot of this every day, so make sure ye boil it so it's ready," he ordered and began showing me how much I should use. On the kitchen table, I noticed a chest expander and a Bullworker. George told me that Charles Atlas used a Bullworker, and that it worked for his chest muscles. He explained the difference to me between the chest expanders which you pulled apart and the Bullworker which had to be pushed inward, working different muscles. He sounded obsessed about every little detail and asked if I could see a difference in him after using them.

"Yeah, George! Ye can tell it's starting to work," I lied. He looked pleased with himself and kept feeling the tops of his arms.

"You're right, it is working, I can feel it," he agreed, smiling. He appeared to be in a good mood. I couldn't work out if it was because Sinead had gone or because he felt his exercises were working. Maybe it was both; either way, I wasn't complaining. I hoped it would last and tried to convince myself, once more, that he'd changed. Maybe working off his nervous tension and aggression doing the exercise would mean that he wouldn't need to take it out on me.

George's two younger brothers called by to see us one afternoon after school. They wanted to see what George was up to with all his exercising. He had been going on and on about it at his mother's house, so they had come to see for themselves. George was delighted to show off the bedroom and his new boxing and exercising skills. However, they didn't seem that impressed with all his talking about Bruce Lee and Charles Atlas. When George wasn't watching, I saw them laughing behind his back. They got on with him well enough, but they knew exactly how he was and didn't dare laugh in front of him.

I was back in the kitchen, making some tea for all of us, when I heard George tell his brothers, "Go on, punch me as hard as you can in the stomach; I won't feel a thing! I'll prove to ye that pain is all in the mind."

I could tell they didn't want to go along with his act. They knew he was no Bruce Lee, and they were worried he might get annoyed with them if they punched him too hard.

"No, George, sure we don't want to punch ye, let it go now," Ed urged.

George, though, wouldn't take no for an answer and wanted to prove to his brothers how tough he was. He kept insisting they punch him so that he could prove what he had been preaching to them. I returned with the tea just in time to see Ron, nearly as big as George at age fourteen, take his most brutal punch. George was obviously winded, though he fought hard not to let it show on his face. He lifted his tea from the table and sat down trying to act like it hadn't affected him; but his face had turned pale, and he was temporarily rooted to his seat.

"See, boys, like I said, it's all in the mind," he insisted, then strolled out heading for the bathroom.

George's brothers grinned at one another, and Ed whispered, "He felt that, Ron. Sure, ye could tell he was in agony."

"Well, he shouldn't have forced me into it." We all laughed and waited for George to return.

A few minutes later, George reappeared, convinced he'd done a great job of fooling all of us. "Ye have to train your mind to do that," he explained to his brothers.

"My God, that's brilliant, George; I wish I could do that. Show us something else that ye can do, George," Ed suggested, playing along with his older brother and pretending to believe him. I don't know how they both managed to keep a straight face because I had to leave the room in fear of George seeing the grin on my face.

I went into the garden with the girls and played with them briefly until Ron and Ed came out. Their mouths were covered with their hands to stop themselves from laughing. "What's going on?" I whispered to them, not wanting George to hear.

"George is going to jump from the bedroom window to prove to us that he won't feel a thing. He's not right in the bloody head," Ed whispered.

I was sure he'd finally gone mad. As I scanned around the part of the garden where he might land, I could see broken bricks and stones scattered about, left over from the building work. When I saw George open the top window and climb onto the windowsill, without his shoes, I took the girls inside and made them comfortable in front of the television, closing the living room door behind me, unsure of what might happen next.

Looking out of the kitchen window, I could see Ed biting his lip to stop himself laughing while Ron tried to talk George out of jumping. George must have stood there for ten minutes or more, acting like he was in a trance. I think he was trying to find the courage to jump. I was quite sure he would go through with it rather than have his brothers think he was all talk.

When he finally jumped, I held my breath and didn't want to look. I was hoping that we wouldn't have to take him to the hospital and explain what had happened. Once again, it was obvious to all of us that he was in terrible pain. He sat for a few moments on the ground, then got himself to his feet and walked into the house, pretending it was no problem at all. It was a relief that he was in one piece with no bones broken. When Ron and Ed left to go home for their dinner, George appeared to be delighted with his performance. He got himself to his feet and hobbled upstairs to take a long soak in the bath.

A few days later, when his new friend, Jerry, came to pick him up, George was drinking another mug of water from the soya bean pan. Jerry told him it looked and smelt awful. George said that people would understand when he ended up with the perfect body! He told him it would be worth it that he would do whatever he had to get it.

Jerry didn't seem at all interested in the subject. "Are ye ready for a wee drink then, George?" he asked. George finished the soya water and, limping slightly, he left with Jerry.

Dog food pie

I woke suddenly to the sound of knocking on my front door. Rubbing the sleep from my eyes, I looked at the alarm clock, and it was five-thirty in the morning. The banging continued, so I rushed downstairs, hoping to open the door before the noise woke the girls.

Jerry was propping up George against the door frame as he was unable to stand on his own. He apologised to me for all the banging and said George couldn't find his keys. I told him not to worry; once Jerry and I had got George comfortably into bed, we sat in the kitchen, drinking coffee and talking until the girls awoke for breakfast.

I liked Jerry, he was a nice person. He had meet George at the pub recently. Even though he had started hanging about with George, he couldn't understand how I had put up with him for so long: acting like he was single. I explained that I didn't have a choice. However, he still suggested that I might be better off if it were just me and the girls. He was genuinely concerned for us. Maybe he suspected that there was more going on as he told me that if I ever needed help or a lift, to the hospital or anywhere else, I was to get a message to him. He gave me his family's address which wasn't too far away.

He liked children and seemed to enjoy being around the girls. He told me he came from a large Catholic family and, as the oldest, he was well used to being around younger children. We all got on well, and I was pleased that we would be seeing him again.

A few days later, Nula pulled up in a taxi and warned me that George was coming home. "He should be here in about ten minutes," she said.

"Oh no, Nula, I've got nothing for his dinner; he won't be too happy about that!"

"I'll see what I've got in." She rushed next door to have a look.

I hadn't expecting George home as he was usually in the pub until much later. He had taken any money we had to the pub, leaving me with nothing to buy food with, but that would not be any excuse when he came home hungry. He wouldn't like being told he'd spent all the food money on drink.

Nula returned, saying she didn't have much because they needed to go shopping, and all she could find was a few tins of dog food and five big spuds. "That will have to do then if there's nothing else!" I surprised myself with what came into my mind, but I was desperate. Nula, looks surprised too, but ran off to get the food while I put the oven on to heat.

She returned with two large tins of dog food with marrowbone. I wasn't sure what that was, but I emptied it into a deep tin pie dish, shoved it in the oven and returned the empty tins to Nula. Who was watching out for George. I put a saucepan of water on to boil and quickly peeled the potatoes, cut them small, and placed them in the pan.

"He's coming now, Frances! I hope you know what you're doing," she warned and giggled to herself as she rushed out of the back door.

George let himself in. "I need to get changed and have something to eat before I head out again. I'll be off for a wee drink with Brian and Jerry in about an hour," he shouted. Then he ran upstairs for a quick bath and a change of clothing. By the time he was ready, I'd mashed the potatoes, covered the meat and put the pie tin back in the oven.

I served George the dog food pie with a small tin of baked beans. I had no idea how it would taste and was worried he might throw the dinner at me or ask what the hell it was. I didn't dare look at him as he tucked into it, as I worried that my expression would give me away. For a few minutes, he ate the food without any comment. I was still afraid to look over at him.

"This is lovely; you can make it more often," he said. Where did you get the meat from?"

I told him Mrs McConnell called in, and she gave it to me as she'd bought too much for the family.

"Ye'll have to be asking her what butchers she used because that was just grand."

"I will be George." I couldn't believe he liked it and couldn't help but smile at the thought of him eating dog food. Perhaps I should be making it more often, I thought! After everything he'd put me through, it wasn't exactly justice, but it felt great.

The next day, I called at Nula's house to thank her and tell her that George had enjoyed his dinner. We sat down and had a good laugh about it. "It's a shame ye can't get away from George. That's no life for ye, fearing him coming home drunk or in a bad mood." I agreed but couldn't see what I could do about it.

Then, the conversation switched to her and Mark and how much they loved each other. I knew she had her worries, with him being English, but I envied her and wished I was as happy. She told me he was becoming increasingly paranoid about getting shot and that he'd been sleeping with a loaded gun under his pillow since leaving the Army.

"Last night, he had a nightmare. When I woke, he had the gun pointed at my head, thinking I was a member of the I.R.A., come to kill him."

"Oh my God, Nula! Are you okay?"

"He frightened the bloody life out of me, Frances. When I saw the gun pointing straight at me, sweat dripping down his face, and him panicking, I thought it was the end for me. I was so scared and was sure he wouldn't wake up. I thought about poor wee Sean, who'd be left without a mother, and how Mark would struggle to live on when he discovered he'd killed me. Then, suddenly, he was wide awake and just as terrified as me."

"I still can't believe how close he came to shooting me, Frances. He's promised he won't sleep with the gun anymore; we'll keep it in the drawer from now on. We can't get rid of it, Frances, because we might need to protect ourselves. It's not safe here for us now. The Troubles just keep getting worse."

I was shocked to hear that Mark had a gun, but I couldn't blame him for wanting to protect himself and his family.

The ordeal had shaken Nula, but she tried to put a brave face on. She told me that Mark wanted them to move to England, but she couldn't bear to be away from her family. I said I'd miss her if she went but that, if I were in her shoes, I would go for their child's sake. Before I left, Nula gave me more tins of food and milk but no dog food. She said that she couldn't help thinking about me when she'd been shopping that morning. "I'm grateful to ye, Nula. It should see me through until I get my family allowance."

That night, after I'd gotten the girls to bed, I put the television on, and the news reported more killings and riots. I had to turn it off because it made me worry even more about my children's safety. I felt depressed with all the misery the Troubles had brought, and my heart went out to my neighbour. I knew that her fears must have been far worse than mine. I had no idea what it felt like to have peace, but I longed for it. To wake up without a care in the world must be incredible. I knew some people lived that way, and I envied them.

It was past midnight when I told myself to stop thinking and worrying about all the misery and get off to bed. I forced myself to think about the good things in my life and pictured my daughters playing happily together. Soon, I drifted off to sleep.

The Explosion

Instantly, I was wide awake, sitting bolt upright in bed and paralysed with fear! The explosion seemed to have come from downstairs. Karen dashed into my bedroom, frightened, and jumped in beside me.

"What was that big noise, Mammy!" she asked.

Deborah was crying so I ran to pick her up and placed her on my bed next to her sister. "Stay there, wee darlings, and don't move until I get back."

Terrified, I crept downstairs to investigate. George was sound asleep in one of the living room chairs. The noise hadn't disturbed him, but I wasn't surprised: I could already smell the alcohol on him.

Entering the kitchen, I could scarcely believe my eyes. What a mess! The gas ring was full on, and meat and gravy were splattered all over the walls and ceiling. The remains of exploded tin can lay on the kitchen floor, a testament to George's haphazard attempt at cooking. Clearly, he had come home hungry, put the tin on the gas without bothering to open it or put transfer it to a saucepan. Then fallen asleep in living room.

After turning off the gas I went back upstairs to reassure the girls and coax them back to sleep. Exhausted, I went back to bed. I was far too tired to start cleaning the mess now, but also, I wanted George to see what he'd done.

When I took the girls down for breakfast that morning, George sat in the kitchen with a cup of tea, looking dishevelled and irritable. "What the hell happened in here," he demanded, surveying the chaos.

"You did that, George, during the night. Ye must have put a tin of meat on the cooker without opening it, and it exploded everywhere,"

He looked at me like I was out of my mind. "Don't ye be so bloody stupid. Sure, I wouldn't have done something like that. Don't you go blaming me for your stupidity." he shouted. He obviously couldn't or didn't want to remember what he'd done.

"I didn't do this, George," I yelled back at him. "The explosion woke us up scared the girls."

Karen tried to defend me and told him, "Daddy, the bang woke me up, and I ran into Mammy's bed."

George looked furious and snapped at her to be quiet before storming out to the garden. From the window, I watched as he lit a cigarette and paced back and forth on the path, seeming unsure of what to do with himself. Eventually, he walked off. I wasn't sure where he'd gone and, to be honest I didn't care. He hated being wrong about anything and despised any hint of criticism. Meanwhile I busied myself getting the children fed and ready for their bath.

Suddenly, George stormed back in, shouting, "When ye finish with them, ye better get that bloody mess in the kitchen cleaned up. What sort of wife are ye anyway? Ye should have got me something to eat last night."

I couldn't help but think that he sounded just like his mother. I couldn't believe what he was saying. I hadn't even known he'd come home. Perhaps he'd been scanning the house for drinking money. Anyways, there was no point trying to argue with him: it would only make matter worse.

"Yeah, I'll do it when the girls are dressed," I said. George stomped off to bed, leaving us all hoping he'd would wake up in a better mood.

By now, the meat had dried hard onto the walls, and it would take a lot of scrubbing to remove it. I let Karen and Deborah play on the floor, where I could keep a watchful eye on them. I couldn't risk letting them get too noisy and waking their father, especially with the mood he was in.

I felt angry and upset that there was one set of rules for him, because he was a man, and different rules for me. I wished he would get up and go out: everything was so tense when he was home.

Balancing on the sink and worktops, I tried to reach the top of the wall and ceiling. I felt exhausted and was too small to reach some of the mess on the ceiling. The mop reached the bit I couldn't get by hand, but it was a slow process. Next, I started on the cooker. It took the better part of the day before the kitchen looked presentable again. George descended the stairs just as I settled with a cup of tea.

"I'm glad to see you've nothing to do but sit around like a lazy bitch," he snarled. "Ye couldn't even keep Deborah quiet. I kept hearing her when I was trying to sleep. Ye have no bloody consideration!"

I started crying with anger. "I'm not a lazy bitch!" I yelled. "I've been cleaning and looking after the girls since ye went to bed, and I've just sat down this minute."

"How hard can it be to keep the house clean and look after a few children, for God's sake? Other people seem to manage it just fine!" he screamed back at me. The girls started crying, and he clenched his fist at us and shouted for us all to shut the fuck up and give his head some fucking peace. I took the children to the living room and hugged them.

"It's all right now, mammy's here. Everything will be alright," I said, trying to comfort them. I wanted to do everything for them but didn't know how. Somehow, I needed to find a way to get them and myself away from him, to forge a better life. I thought that maybe I just hadn't been thinking hard enough. There had to be a way out and I needed to do it soon.

Just then, George called me to make him something to eat. He was still in an awful mood, so I was relieved when he said he would be leaving in a while. I tried to ignore his grumblings and went to the cupboard to see what was there.

"Ye haven't even boiled my soya beans, ye fucking lazy bitch. I told ye, I need them every day. You're fucking useless!" he shouted and jumped up. Then bang! The side of my head seemed to explode, and I collapsed in a heap. I tried to get up and explain that I'd had to clean the cooker, but he lashed out at me again just as I reached my feet. I caught his fist on my arm, knocking me back to the floor. Then I saw his foot coming for me. I tried to move, but he got me in the back, and I cried out in agony.

"Stop it, George. I'll lose the baby if ye don't stop. I'm pregnant, George and I will lose this child," thinking that this would make him come to his senses.

"Ye bloody deserved that, ye wee bitch, now get me some fucking food!" he demanded and slapped me across the face.

Karen was at the kitchen door screaming, "Leave my mammy alone, stop it, Daddy," she cried. George ordered her back to sit in the living room until his food was ready.

She'd seen it all happen this time. I couldn't stop him. I could hear her sobbing and called out to her, "I'm all right now Karen; I'll be in with ye soon." I was in agony and wept as I prepared his food. I hated him for putting us through this hell. I wanted better for my children and felt like I was failing them.

George sat at the table, waiting for his food as if he was Lord of the Manor and I was his servant. I was so angry that I wanted to kill him. I thought about stabbing him with the kitchen knife. Then I came to my senses: I knew I couldn't do it with my children in the house. Also, the thought of going to prison and not being with them was too much for me to bear. I wanted him out of my life and wished he were dead because I couldn't see any other way to escape from him.

George ate his meal and told me to put cold water on my face before Brian and Jerry turned up. "I don't want ye looking like that and showing me up. Ye should have done what I told ye, and ye wouldn't have got me annoyed. As I told you before, pain is all in the mind; don't think about it."

I couldn't believe what he was saying. My sister was right about him. She'd always called him a crazy bastard and was convinced he wasn't right in the head.

The door knocked, and it sounded like Jerry and Brian. The moment he saw me, Jerry knew that something was wrong. "Are ye okay, Frances? Ye don't look too well," he said as I placed a mug of tea before him.

"She's fine," George insisted. I forced a smile and left the kitchen. George talked about his bodybuilding and got Brian and Jerry to feel how tight his arm muscles were. I thought everyone must be fed up with that conversation by now - I know I was. Maybe they were too polite to tell him to, "Shut the hell up!" or they feared how he would react.

As soon as they left for the pub, Nula knocked on the door. "I was waiting for him to go out, Frances. Are you all right? I heard ye screaming earlier." She knew I wasn't okay the minute she saw me. I couldn't speak and just burst into tears. She walked me to the kitchen, put the kettle on and got me a cup of tea.

The girls went into the garden to play now that their dad had gone. I removed my blouse and showed Nula the bruising that George had left. A large lump was also forming on my head behind my right ear. "Ye better get something cold on that, Frances," she suggested. She got a tea towel and ran it under the cold water tap. "Here, Frances, that should help with the swelling," she said, pressing the cold towel against my head.

Tears dripped into the cup as I sipped the tea. I was inconsolable and needed to cry it all out of my system. She was furious when I eventually calmed down and told her what had happened.

"Ye can't stay with that bastard any longer, Frances. He doesn't give a shit about ye. He's of down the pub enjoying himself, just like nothing happened."

"Yeah, I know I have to do something, but what? He knows I've got nowhere to go. I wish he'd die and give us all some peace. I hate him!" I heard a knock at the door and got up to answer it. Nula hid in the back garden in case it was George coming back so she would escape next door.

"Can I come in a wee minute?" Jerry asked. "I told George I had something to do once I'd dropped him and Brian off at the pub. Don't worry, Frances: he doesn't know I'm here." I was surprised to see him and realised I must have looked like a hopeless mess, with my eyes all puffed up and red from crying. I walked him to the kitchen and called Nula in from the garden.

"It's all right, Nula, thankfully, it's not George." I introduced her to Jerry and put the kettle on to make a fresh pot of tea.

"Will ye sit down there, Frances, and I'll make the tea." Nula insisted.

"What's been going on here?" Jerry asked.

I didn't answer him immediately, unsure where to start the conversation. This was George's drinking partner. I wasn't sure what to tell him, but Nula had no problem blurting out everything to this friend of George. She explained what he was doing to me when no one was around to see it. "He needs locking up if you ask me!" she claimed.

Jerry looked genuinely concerned for me and said he had no idea George was like that. He knew something was wrong earlier, and that's why he came back. He wanted to see if I was okay.

"I thought it was bad enough that he was always out enjoying himself and leaving Frances to cope alone with the wee ones. I didn't know he was a wife-beater," he assured Nula.

"Ye should try living next door to him: then you'd know. We hear it all through the walls. He's a bastard, Jerry; that's what he is." Nula sounded very angry.

Just then, Karen came in to tell me that she and Deborah wanted to watch the television. Jerry picked her up and sat her down on his knee while I went to get Deborah. None of us mentioned George, while the girls were about. However, Karen did tell Jerry that her daddy was bad, and he shouldn't hurt her mammy. I could tell that Jerry was shocked by what he'd heard and showed genuine concern for me and the girls.

When the girls were fed and washed, Nula took them to her house to play with Sean. "Come on round when you're ready, Frances," she said on her way out the back door.

Jerry quizzed me some more about what was going on with George. "I might be his friend, ye know, but what he's doing to ye isn't right," his voice sounded sad but comforting. "Nobody knows what he is like, Frances; it's a shock. I don't know how I will be able to look him in the face again, without punching him."

"Jerry, I really don't want to talk about it." I felt embarrassed that I couldn't deal with the problem myself. I knew George would go completely mad if Jerry took my side and stopped being his friend. Jerry sensed my concern and assured me he wouldn't tell George we'd spoken.

After Jerry left, I found myself sitting alone in the kitchen, succumbing to tears that had been building up inside me for far too long. The situation had become unbearable, not just for me but also for my daughters. Yet, despite the overwhelming weight of it all, I couldn't see a clear path forward.

The thought of involving the police crossed my mind, but I knew all too well that they often turned a blind eye to domestic disputes. If it weren't for the welfare of my children, I would have fled without a second thought, leaving George far behind. The idea of roughing it on my own didn't faze me but with the children to consider that just wasn't possible and with no family to turn to I had nowhere else to go. Also, if I found a way out, I was terrified to think what might happen if he managed to catch up with me. It seemed impossible to be thinking about leaving him.

"Come on, Frances, pull yourself together," I told myself. I got up and tried to tidy myself up before going next door. The cold water from the tap cooled my face and head, which was still throbbing. I waited until the blotchy red patches around my eyes had faded before facing my girls. I wanted them to feel that everything was okay. I took a few deep breaths and headed around the back of Nula's house. I could hear Karen laughing, and I hurried in the back door to give her and Deborah a big kiss and a hug.

The Last Rights

Over the next six months, I lived to exist for my children and no more than that. I was getting through one day at a time, whatever it brought. I had no choice but to try and make the best of things. My feelings towards George grew increasingly bitter, but I tried not to show them. Everything I did was done in a robot fashion. I felt as though a large part of myself was already dead. George carried on as usual, thinking only of his wants and needs.

Whenever he came home drunk and left a few more bruises on me, he'd claim later that he couldn't remember because he was drunk, as if that made it okay! Somehow, he always managed to find the money for the pub, but, more often now, there was little, or nothing left to buy food. Not that it would have stopped him from expecting a meal whenever he came home. We had become increasingly dependent on handouts.

Whenever she called to see me, Mrs McConnell would bring money, food, and clothes for the children, and Nula and some of my other neighbours would give me things. I would have saved everything I had for the children to eat, but I knew my unborn child needed nourishment. I hid any food or money that came our way, so George wouldn't find it. I knew he wouldn't starve as he constantly got fed at his mother's house.

"Oh George, are ye hungry," she would say to him. "I see that wee bitch isn't feeding ye up, son. I told ye that one wouldn't make ye good wife." I had to hold myself back from telling her what I thought, as I knew it would only make things worse.

I was eight months pregnant and relieved to have only a month to go. It seemed that I must either be carrying a larger baby or, as the doctor told me, a lot of fluid. Whatever the reason, I was huge! Sitting down and getting up was very uncomfortable, and I had a lot of pain and discomfort in my back. I don't suppose my lifestyle helped!

It was the last week of January 1975, and the weather was cold and wet. I didn't venture out with the girls much: they either played in the house or we'd go next door for a while.

One evening, as I sat in the living room after a day spent at Nula's, I was startled by noises emanating from the back of the house. The sound resembled someone stumbling against the bin in the rear garden. I was too frightened to go to the kitchen and look out the window because it was dark and George never used the back door. It was much easier to use the front.

Another crash followed, jolting me into action as I feared for my children. My mind raced to the darkest possibilities. Perhaps it was the IRA, mistaking my home for Mark's. Without hesitation, I bolted out the front door and urgently knocked on Nula's. She dashed off to retrieve Mark's gun from their bedroom, returning in a matter of seconds, ready to confront whatever threat lurked outside.

"Go on in. I'm right here with ye," she said, pushing me through the door.

I stood in the hall and listened. There was another sound, and I looked around for Nula. "Did ye hear that?" I whispered.

"Nula, you're not with me: you're way behind me!"

She checked the gun over and appeared to know what she was doing. I imagined her husband would have shown her how to protect herself if he was not around.

"All ye have to do now is aim it at the door and pull the trigger hard if someone comes through it," she said, handing me the gun. "Don't think about it, Frances, just do it, or it might be too late!"

I was surprised by how heavy it was. As I thought about my children asleep in their beds upstairs, I knew Nula was right. The only feelings I had now were to protect my daughters. It seemed a drastic thing to do, but we weren't living in normal times. On the news, we regularly heard of people being shot in their homes by the IRA or some other organisation. I was terrified at the thought of what might happen and the realisation that I might kill someone. Shaking with fear, I gripped the gun with both hands to steady myself. When I heard someone trying the back door handle, I froze, knowing the door was unlocked.

Who's there? What do you want?" I yelled. The door creaked open, and in the dimness of the kitchen, I made out the outline of a man stumbling inside. "What do you want?" I shouted again, my finger tightening on the trigger. I had him in my sights when suddenly he found the light switch, illuminating the kitchen. It took a moment for my brain to register that it was George, drunk as usual. I still had the gun aimed at his chest. He sobered up quickly once he saw the gun in my hand. He wasn't being cocky now and probably thought that I had finally had enough of him; that I had acquired the gun from someone with the intention to shoot him for all he had put me and the girls through.

"What the fuck do ye think you're doing? Are ye mad or what? Put the gun down." He sounded sober now and panicked.

I could feel Nula's hand on my arm now, "It's okay, Frances, it's only George."

The gun remained pointed directly at his chest. I thought to pull the trigger anyway. If I could get away with it, it would eliminate all my problems immediately. My heart raced, my mouth became parched, and I broke out in a cold sweat.

"Just do it. Shoot the bastard!" the voice in my head was shouting at me.

George didn't move and looked terrified of what I might do. Perhaps he realised what I was thinking. Time seemed to have stood still, and it felt like we had been frozen in that position for ages when it was probably only seconds. Again, the voice persisted, "Go on, Frances, just do it now, don't think about it. Do it for your daughters, or ye will miss your chance." I could feel my finger tightening on the trigger and a sick feeling in my stomach. Something was holding me back: the moment had gone, and I couldn't do it. I took a deep breath and lowered the gun. Nula reached out and took it from me.

He sat on a kitchen chair, his face pale and staring at me like he knew I wanted to kill him.

"Ye crazy bitch, Ye could have bloody shot me." George began shouting. Nula told him that we both thought he was the IRA or someone like that.

"Who the hell are you, and what are ye doing in my house?"

"Ye frightened the life out of us, George." I tried to explain! "Ye, never come to the back door. I had to knock for the neighbour. Anyway, it wasn't a real gun: it was just a water pistol belonging to next door's wee boy."

I knew that I had to convince George that the gun wasn't real. Not because I didn't want to think that I wouldn't have shot him, but if he knew they had a gun next door then word would get out and that would draw attention to Mark, which was the last thing they needed. Fortunately, in his drunken state, he believed me about the water pistol saying,

"Yeah, where the fuck would someone like, you get a real gun from. I knew all along what it was all along," he boasted.

He sat on a kitchen chair, his face pale and contorted with confusion. Nula went home with the gun, and I ran upstairs to check on the girls, who were still fast asleep. I kissed them and closed their bedroom door. George, who had followed me upstairs now, grabbed me with both hands around my neck. The stench of whisky on him made me feel nauseous and I tried to refrain from throwing up. I was terrified.

"Did ye tell those nosy neighbours our private business, Frances?" It was the first time he'd used my name in a long while, I had started to think my name was Bitch.

He was furious, and I could sense trouble brewing. It was his usual pattern when he got like this. Before I could even comprehend what was happening, he had pushed me and I was tumbling down the stairs. As I hit the bottom in a painful heap, a sharp jolt shot up my back, rendering me immobile. While I sat there, waiting for the pain to subside, George stood at the top of the stairs, hurling curses and insults my way. Moments later, as I attempted to get up, I realised I was sitting in a puddle of water.

"Oh no, my water had broken!" I cried out. It was a month earlier than expected, and I couldn't help but worry what that might mean for the baby.

Just then, there was a knock on the door, and George ordered me to be quiet while he answered it. "We don't want everybody knowing our business, now do we?" he snarled. He opened the door a fraction, blocking the view into the hall.

"All right, George," Jerry's voice said and George kept him talking at the door for a while. Then I heard him say he'd be out in a wee minute, and they could go to the pub.

"I'll just use your toilet before we go," Jerry insisted, following George through the door. I was still sitting on the floor at the bottom of the stairs, and George acted surprised to see me there.

"Oh my god, Frances, have ye slipped on those stairs again," he said, coming to help me.

I was embarrassed to be seen sitting in a puddle of water as if I'd wet myself. Jerry said nothing but looked concerned as he walked past me to the bathroom. I didn't believe that he needed the toilet. He probably just wanted to see if I was okay. George's behaviour, keeping him at the door, must have made him suspicious. George got me to a chair in the kitchen and quickly mopped the floor up before Jerry appeared back downstairs.

"She's fine now, Jerry. She just slipped down the last few stairs. I'm always telling her to take it easy." George grabbed his coat from the hall. "Come on then, let's be off."

It was a great relief to me that George had gone out. I couldn't have taken much more abuse from him, so maybe Jerry turning up like that was a godsend. My back ached as I hobbled around the kitchen, making myself a cup of hot, sweet tea. Someone had once told me it was good for shock. I wasn't getting any contractions yet, so I thought I would sit and think about what to do. It was at least two miles to the hospital, and I knew I wouldn't be in a fit state to walk it. I didn't have a phone to ring for an ambulance and the nearest phone box would be too far away. I tried to think of all the people I knew with a car who would drive me, but I gave up as there was no way of contacting them.

Then, I thought about George out enjoying himself while I was left worrying about what to do if I went into labour. It made me so angry that I began to wish I had shot him. I knew that he wouldn't tell anyone my waters had broken or send any help. It would spoil his drinking time: people might tell him that he should be at home with his wife and kids. He would have hated that.

I thought of going next door, but I held off momentarily as I felt that Nula and Mark had been dragged into my problems enough lately, and they could probably use a break. I told myself I would only knock on their door if it became essential.

An hour or so passed while I sat in the kitchen trying to figure out what to do next. The pain in my back was worsening when I heard someone knocking on the front door. It made me think that George had found some mercy and returned to get me to the hospital. However, when I answered the door and saw it wasn't George, I felt stupid for once again thinking he would ever change. It was Mary, a lady I knew just to say hello when we met on the street. She told me that Jerry had called and asked if she would see if I was okay. "He sounded concerned," she explained.

I asked her to come in for a moment. The pains in my back wouldn't allow me to stand there for much longer. She immediately realised that I was in quite a bad way and, taking my arm, helped me walk back into the kitchen. "Jerry asked me not to say anything to George about coming to see ye. I think he should be here to look after ye, Frances. Would you like me to find him for ye?" I was sure my heart had missed a few beats, and I begged her not to.

"He already knows," I told her.

"So, what's been going on here then?" she asked. I broke down in floods of tears, and Mary went to put on the kettle. I was afraid to say anything because she knew George's family well, and I was sure this would get back to them. Also, I was convinced she wouldn't believe me even if I could tell her. Why on earth did Jerry send her, I thought?

Didn't he realise how impossible this was going to be for me to explain?

Mary sat next to me and handed me a mug of tea. "There ye go now, get that into ye, and you'll feel much better. Now, what is it? Have ye had a bit of a falling out with George? Well, it happens to all couples, ye know. I'm sure he'll be back soon enough to make it up to ye."

She sounded kind and like she meant well. She was in her late twenties and had two children, a boy and a girl. Her husband, Barry, was a lovely family man and very good to her and the children. Whenever I saw them together, they always looked so happy. I told her we had a bit of a disagreement and that, after he left, I fell down the stairs, and my waters broke. I told her I didn't want her to get him because he might blame himself for my falling.

"He's staying at his mother's house tonight. I would rather leave him there until I get checked out by a doctor."

"Okay then, I'll take ye to the hospital. I have the car outside. If ye get the girls ready, they can stay at my house. Another two won't make any difference. My husband will watch them while we're at the hospital. Now, that's settled, let's get you ready." There was nothing I could do but accept her offer, so I went to get the girls.

We didn't have to wait long to see a doctor who said that I would have to stay as the baby could be born any time now. When Mary told me that she would have to tell Mrs McAteer, or they would be concerned, I begged her not to say that Jerry asked her to call in on me as he would get into trouble.

"I know Jerry very well. He wouldn't have asked me to do this if it wasn't important. So, although I don't like to lie, I'll tell George's mother that I saw you outside your door. I was passing by and stopped to help as ye didn't look too well. But I'll have to go to confession on Friday for my sins!" she said, half joking.

I was sure that she suspected there was more going on than I had told her, but I couldn't worry about that now. I was grateful to Mary and Barry especially as I knew that the girls would be well looked after at their house for the night.

The following morning, I woke at six o'clock to the sound of the tea trolley. "Frances, there's a wee cup of tea for ye." the tea lady said.

I felt a bit disappointed that I had not given birth yet. There was still a lot of pain in my back, but I must have been so tired that I slept through it. Five other ladies were in the ward, three of whom had contractions and two who had gone over their time and were waiting to be induced.

Three doctors had prodded at my stomach that morning, listening for the baby's heartbeat with what looked like a plastic horn. They all said it wouldn't be long now, and I should expect to have the baby by that evening. The day dragged by, and all I could do was to worry about George and how he would react when I next saw him. The other women were taken off to the delivery rooms, one by one, to have their babies, but there was no change with me. I lay there all day in discomfort, waiting for my contractions to start and wondering if my baby was all right. It would soon be nearly a whole day since my waters had broken.

Unfortunately, there were no visitors to help the time pass. It was a relief, though, that George hadn't turned up. I thought about my girls, and soon, tears were dripping onto the pillow. I wasn't used to being away from them for so long. I wanted them with me to give them a big hug.

The following morning, I was still waiting for my contractions. The doctors looked more worried and kept coming back to check on me. I was weak, and they struggled to find the baby's heartbeat. They seemed even more concerned, and I heard one of them say that if the baby didn't come that night, they would have to do a caesarean. I wished they could tell me what was happening and why my baby wasn't born yet. At one point, I woke up to find a priest standing over me, a candle burning on my locker and the curtains drawn as he administered the last rites.

Then, thankfully, I was in labour, but with my waters having broken so long ago, the birth was truly horrendous. Even with the gas and air, the pain was unbearable, and the contractions seemed to go on forever.

When the priest returned, the following morning, he seemed shocked that we were both still alive. "It's truly a miracle," he said, then blessed himself. He prayed there silently for a moment. "Bless you, Frances, he's a beautiful wee child. I expect I will see you very soon about the baptism."

The gypsy had been right, about it being a boy. My sister-in-law, Angela, had been brought in during the night also and had given birth to a baby girl. They put her in the bed next to mine, assuming we would want to be close to one another. The truth was that I hadn't met her before. She was Frank's wife, and they didn't associate with us.

However, we did get talking in the hospital as there wasn't much else, we could do.

We talked about baby names, and I told her that if I'd had a girl I would have called her Corinna. She said it was a beautiful name, and she told me that her choice for a boy would have been Leon. I loved the name, and we decided to use each other's choices.

The following day, the registrar came to the ward asking if we wanted our babies registered. The cost was one shilling and Angela kindly gave me the money. I was delighted to know that my son would not be grow up with a name like Bruce Lee.

Internment

Sinead had visited me on a few occasions and told me that she was still looking for a flat for us in Belfast. There were plenty about, she said, however finding one that would allow me to have the children was proving difficult. She promised to keep looking though, and maybe she would get lucky.

A few weeks later, when a white Cortina pulled up outside the house, I was understandably nervous. But then, the passenger door swung open and Sinead's excited figure emerged and rushed towards my front door.

"Good news, Frances! I think I've found a place for you in Belfast. Hopefully, you can leave that bastard behind and make a new life for you and the kids. I've a friend who's giving us a lift, but you have to come with me now, to Belfast. Come on, Frances, pack a bag with whatever you need for the wee ones, and I'll help ye get them into the car."

My head spun with a mixture of excitement and confusion; her visit had been completely unexpected. I dashed around the living room gathering up nappies, clothes, bottles and baby food and crammed them all into a bag. Within moments of Sinead's arrival, we were on our way: the baby nestled on my lap and the girls, either side of me, engrossed in their books. Fortunately, George had gone out fishing earlier that morning so I was reasonably confident that he wouldn't return before we got back home.

Sinead introduced me to Conner, the driver, explaining that he was a friend. He was polite and friendly with a thick Belfast accent. He didn't say much but that may have been because Sinead filled the journey with chatter. She was enthusiastic about the prospect of us living close to each other and longed to see the children and me liberated from George's clutches. Though uncertainties loomed, I began to feel hopeful for a fresh start.

We halted outside a bustling pub, to stretch our legs, and Conner suggested that we go inside as it belonged to a friend of the family. Inside, Irish music was playing, and Karen decided that she was going to dance. Deborah watched on and smiled as Karen entertained her.

Our presence attracted curious glances from some of the regular patrons, but they seemed friendly enough. Sinead ordered drinks and crisps from the bar and led us to a table. Meanwhile, Connor conversed with the barman before disappearing behind the bar to make a call. Sinead and Karen selected some songs from the jukebox and then Karen continued to dance.

I pondered our situation, impatiently, as we waited for news of the person who could, potentially, help us find a new home. What sort of a person was he and would there be any strings attached? When Sinead returned with Karen, I asked her about her friend.

"Aiden's a good person, ye don't need to be worrying about him. I think Connor is talking to him right now so we should be going to meet with him soon." Her words offered some comfort in that respect. Although, nagging away at the back of my mind was the constant worry that George might return home earlier than expected and discover my absence. However, there was nothing I could do about that now.

I felt that we have travelled a considerable distance only to find ourselves stalled in uncertainty. So, I was pleased when Connor returned, a few minutes later, to say, "We have to go now, Frances. Aiden is at his mother's house and we're to meet him there. It's just a few minutes' drive up the road."

Sinead offered to take the children to her flat to play and have some food while Conner took me to see Aiden. It seemed like a sensible idea, so we dropped them off on the way and I then settled into the passenger seat beside Connor.

Without Sinead, conversation flowed more freely as we made our way. Connor told me that he had only recently discovered that Sinead had a sister, when she had been talking about her experiences growing up in the convent.

"I'm so sorry," he said "That you had to suffer all that torment with those bastard nuns. I went to school with the Christian Brothers. Those priests could be just as bad so I know what it must have been like for you both, Frances. I could tell you some awful stories about what happened to some friends of mine. Those nuns and priests are a lot of fuckers, if you ask me, Frances!" Connors voice was tinged with sadness as he went on to recount some of those ordeals.

Arriving at a house, with a young boy waving enthusiastically from the front garden, Connor confirmed that we were at Aiden's who had just stepped out of the house and was now approaching us with a warm, friendly smile. He invited us into the house, and I felt instantly at ease in his company.

Inside the house buzzed with lively conversation and laughter and the enticing aroma of a traditional roast dinner wafted in from the kitchen. Aiden introduced me to his siblings and their families who exuded warmth and hospitality. His mother emerged from the kitchen, insisting that we stay for dinner, an invitation which, out of respect for Irish tradition, I could hardly refuse.

"We'll have a wee chat when we've eaten," Aiden suggested as we gathered around the large kitchen table for Sunday roast. Amidst the animated conversation and delicious meal, served up by Aiden's mother, I marvelled at the sense of belonging and acceptance which was such a stark contrast to my own experience. I was completely at ease and able, temporarily, to put aside all my own worries. I could scarcely imagine what it would be like to be part of a family like this.

"You look like you need feeding up, Frances. Sure, you are way too thin. You need your strength for your wee ones!" insisted Aiden's mother as she piled a few more roast potatoes onto my plate.

The meal and conversation were a welcome distraction from my own life. Then, suddenly and catastrophically, the tranquillity was shattered by a deafening bang which reverberated around the room and shook me to the core. British soldiers burst in through the damaged doorway; their menacing presence sending a shockwave through the room. Cries of fear and confusion filled the air while I sat frozen in disbelief. Meanwhile, other soldiers, who had entered through the front door, were storming upstairs until every corner of the house was infiltrated.

As the soldiers held us at gunpoint, their weapons pointing menacingly directly at us, panic and uncertainty gripped us all. The chaotic sounds, emanating from upstairs, further heightened our sense of dread. I felt my body trembling uncontrollably as I grappled with the terrible prospect of what might happen to me next. Everything occurred so quickly and with such violence that it was impossible to think rationally.

Aiden's mother, visibly distressed and struggling to catch her breath, caused an additional wave of concern for her family. Amidst the chaos and confusion one of her daughters sprang bravely into action, with a soldier's rifle pointed directly at her and demands for her to sit down she frantically retrieving mother's medication from a kitchen drawer. Her back to me, I couldn't see what passed between her and the soldier, but we were all relieved when she was back safely in her seat and had handed the box of tablets to her mother.

Ordered to remain calm and seated: we were powerless to affect our situation. It was at this moment of despair that a realisation of my own mortality washed over me. Tears streamed down my cheeks as I grappled with the unbearable thought of never seeing my children again.

Then, loud footsteps thundered back down the stairs and more soldiers poured into the room. They signalled for Aiden and his brother, Sean, to come to them, but in a desperate bid for freedom Aiden tried to make a break for it. Cries of defiance echoed through the chaos as he fought tooth and nail against his captors. Through the window, I watched in horror, and he was dragged away, his bloodied face a stark testament to his struggle.

Amidst the chaos and despair, sobs and desperate cries of, "Where are you taking them?" echoed throughout the room.

Aiden's mother, her face etched with agony, appeared as though her world had collapsed before her eyes. Witnessing her anguish, I couldn't fathom the depths of pain she must be feeling, and I silently prayed that I would never have to endure such heart-wrenching separation from my children.

The soldiers departed as rapidly as they had arrived, leaving behind a trail of devastation and despair. As their armoured vehicles rumbled away, carrying within them the two brothers, the harsh reality of our precarious existence weighed heavily on us all.

One of Aiden's sisters, visibly shaken by the scene upstairs, urged her mother not to go up and swiftly arranged for her to stay at her own house until they had time to sort everything out. Equally stunned by the events, Connor offered his assistance: promising to return the next day to lend a helping hand.

Guided by Connor's comforting presence, I numbly followed him to the car. Both of us were in too much of a state of shock to go back to the children so Connor stopped off at the pub we had visited earlier to give us time to come to terms with our ordeal. The barman poured us each a double brandy as Connor recounted to him the events of the afternoon.

The brandy, music and welcoming atmosphere all helped to slowly calm my nerves. Talking about the events seemed also to help; inevitably, the conversation revolved around the afternoon's events and the fate of Aiden and his brother. The gravity of their situation weighed heavily on us all.

That the brothers had been taken into internment seemed clear to everyone. It was an all too familiar story. Aiden and his brother seemed such friendly people and I had no idea why the army had taken them. It seemed to many of us that just being Catholic was reason enough. By the time internment was to end, in 1975, almost 2,000 people had been interned: almost all of whom were Catholic. Such a misguided and biased policy did nothing but fuel resentment within the Catholic community probably resulting in even more violence.

The conversation and drink had definitely helped to calm me. Conner, conscious of the need to drive us home, firmly declined any more drinks and now felt that we should be on our way.

By the time we arrived back home, the kids and I were exhausted. Fortunately, despite the late hour, George was still out. I suspected that he was now probably in the pub, after the days fishing, and would probably end up spending the night at his mother's.

Sinead and Connor assisted me in getting the children settled down. Both then agreed to stay with me for a while longer before heading back to Belfast. Their presence was a balm to my still frayed nerves. I loved my sister dearly and was so thankful to have her with me that evening.

The Hotel

After I had finally produced the son George had longed for, I had hoped he would be happier. However, his behaviour towards me had deteriorated rather than improve. I had hoped that our son, Leon, would inspire a positive change in him. After all, George had achieved everything he professed to desire. Yet, disappointingly, fatherhood only seemed to amplify his ego. He boasted to anyone who would listen that he had become a man now that he had a son.

No matter what I did, it seemed to irritate George, so I learned to keep my daily activities to myself. My primary concern remained that of caring for our children to the best of my ability. Meanwhile, I was constantly thinking about how to escape without being detected. My determination to secure a brighter future for my children fuelled my resolve.

George would return home now and then, consumed by paranoia about my activities and would mercilessly taunt me about my appearance. "You used to look stunning; that's why I wanted to marry you. But look at you now; you probably have cancer. Don't expect me to stick around and look after you," he'd sneer.

I had reached my breaking point, and despite the constant threat of physical abuse, there were moments when I couldn't help but snap back at him. "Well, George, if you didn't spend so much on drink, perhaps we could afford some food," I'd counter. It may not have been the wisest decision, but I could no longer suppress my thoughts. George couldn't stand being questioned about his drinking, and he would constantly remind me of a man's entitlement to drink.

In one respect, George was right, and I was extremely underweight. I was so worried about having enough food for my children that I had almost stopped eating.

I was surviving mainly on cups of tea, and whenever Nula was kind enough to leave me some cigarettes, I would have a cigarette with my tea.

Whenever Mrs McConnell would visit, she would bring vegetables and tinned food. Sometimes, she would have clothes that her children had outgrown, and she would always leave twenty-five pounds. "Frances, this is for you and the children; don't let his lordship get his hands on it. Please, make sure you get yourself something to eat."

Without her help, for which I will always be overwhelmingly grateful, I don't know how the children and I would have survived. I hadn't spoken to her about George, but she had figured out for herself what was happening, and I guessed that others had seen through George's facade, too. On the days when she left me some money, I would take the children down to see Kerry at the hotel. Kerry and I had met a few times at the park, and one day, she suggested that the kids and I should come and see her at the hotel where she worked. Sometimes, Nula would go too if Mark was at work. She liked to be at home with him when he was off. We always had a great time, and I got to know Kelly well.

Soon, it had got to the point where I had felt confident to confide fully in Kerry. Although I had imagined she'd already guessed much of what was happening. She was great with my children and often bought them food and drinks. They loved being around her, and she promised to help in any way she could.

My cousins were regularly in the hotel bar, and they would often bring me a drink and ask how I was doing. It was good to see them, but their parents would still not have anything to do with me, or Sinead. Fortunately, I had gotten past their avoidance of me and had begun to feel I didn't ever want to have anything to do with them either, so that was fine.

Karen always liked to help me pick out the songs on the jukebox, usually the same ones. She was now three and a half and the boss of everyone. If anyone shortened her brother's or sister's name, she would correct them in her matter-of-fact voice, as if they were stupid for not saying the names correctly. She had also started calling me Frances instead of Mammy. Whenever she referred to her dad, he was Daddy George. Deborah wasn't so chatty: she had her big sister to say everything for her and boss her around, and that was fine by her.

I somehow managed to keep all of this from George. Karen, who spoke clearly, would often chat about her day. I may have been worried about what George would think if he heard her. But her dad was never around her long enough to be bothered to listen to her gabbling. If he had heard anything, he would probably assume that she was playing a game with her dolls.

George was never going to let me get a divorce from him. The kids and I needed to get somewhere safe. Just a few weeks ago, he had held a knife to my throat and threatened to slash my face if I tried to leave. He had threatened to leave my face in such a mess that no one would ever want to look at me. He was controlling and paranoid and I believed every word. I would have to make sure that he could never catch me if I was ever to escape with the children. Perhaps, in his mind, he felt that me leaving him would be an insult to his manhood. He wouldn't want people thinking that he might have been an awful husband. He didn't cut me with the knife, but by the next morning I was covered in bruises around my neck and face.

George would never accept responsibility for what he had done, and that morning was no different. What the hell's wrong with your face? He would say, did ye have an accident or look at someone the wrong way? Whenever I told him that he'd done it, he'd call me a liar and tell me that I'd better not be telling people things like that, or I might have a bad 'accident!' Then, generally, he would throw me an evil stare and storm off out, if I was lucky!

For days after that beating, Nula would come around and put makeup on my face. Although the bruises were healing, I still needed the touch of concealer on my face before I felt confident enough to go out in public. With the constant bruising and weight loss, I'm sure that people must have had an idea of what was going on but didn't want to intrude.

Life was chaotic, and I always seemed to be busy either looking after the children or sorting out and putting up with their father. All the while, especially during calmer moments of the day, I would be thinking and worrying about how to get away safely.

It had been another one of those lovely days when Mrs McConnell had been to visit. It was always a joy to hear about her children and how they were getting on with their new nanny. This time, she'd brought some vegetables from her garden and some toys and books for the children, all of which were greatly appreciated. Once again, she'd left twenty-five pounds for me and told me to hide it from his lordship. I thanked her and wondered, once more, how I would have coped without her friendship and generosity. Then, I washed and dressed the kids, and we headed out to the hotel to visit Kelly.

I hadn't seen her for a few days, and she didn't hold back with her delight at seeing the children. Drinks and chocolate were quickly followed by huge hugs and kisses. "Aha, it's great to see ye, Frances. I will get ye and the wee ones some sandwiches in a wee minute," she said.

Karen ran to the jukebox, waiting for me to put her favourite songs on. This had become her favourite place. I had brought some of the books and toys from Mrs McConnell, and the girls were kept amused and happy. I went to the bar and ordered some drinks and crisps for my children and me. Before I got a chance to pay, my cousin Johnny, standing at the end of the bar, shouted, "I'll get that." I was beginning to wonder if he ever went home as he seemed to be a permanent fixture at the end of the bar.

Kelly came over to chat and mentioned she had been watching the news. She shared that Gerry Adams had made an appearance, discussing the talks he had been engaged in, aiming for a peaceful resolution. His remarks seemed to offer a glimmer of hope for an end to internment soon. Adams, a member of Sinn Féin, the political arm of the IRA advocating for a united Ireland, was seen as a significant figure in the ongoing negotiations.

I had met him once when he knocked on my door asking me to join the fight against internment by joining the rent strike. Three or four counties in Northern Ireland were already on rent strike, and he wanted us to join them and support the cause. I thought it was a good cause, and he appeared to be a nice person.

Johnny came over and put another drink on the table for me, saying, "Here ye go, Frances, there's a wee drink for ye. That makeup is not covering those bruises too well. I take it George is responsible for doing that to ye?"

"Don't ye worry yourself about me, Johnny. Trust me, I will be leaving him as soon as I can arrange for somewhere else to live, away from Omagh." He told me to look after myself and then returned to the bar. I enjoyed sitting and watching the kids play with their new books and toys. I listened to the music playing on the jukebox and let it wash over me as I enjoyed my drink.

The atmosphere was friendly and, as I listened to all the country and western songs, I thought of a way to frighten George off from beating me up again. If my plan worked, it might keep me safe until I could finally leave him. The next time he tried to use me as a punching bag, I would tell him that I had left a legal letter as insurance with Mr McConnell. It would say that if anything happened to me, and I end up in a hospital or dead, then they should look no further than my husband.

Most people, if that had happened, would guess it was him anyway, but the letter would shine a light on George. He would not like the thought of a letter being out there somewhere where he couldn't get his hands on it. I wouldn't do it, but I knew that he was paranoid enough to believe that I would. The more I sipped my drink, the more the idea appealed to me. Although I knew it wouldn't protect me forever, I was reasonably confident that it would make him think before he raised his hand to me again.

Three young soldiers entered the bar and almost immediately remembered us from the last time we had been there. They waved to us and then came over to say hello. Then, once they had ordered their drinks, they sat at the table closest to ours. They bought some chocolate buttons for the kids, which was very kind of them. I reminded Karen to say thank you, which she willingly did. There was no point in asking Deborah to use her manners as she didn't talk to people, she left Karen to do that for her. They were soon sitting over at the soldier's table, showing them their books. They didn't seem bothered by their intrusion and laughed at Karen bossing Deborah.

As I watched the soldiers interacting with my daughters, I wished their father could have that same connection with his children. I told them to let me know when they'd had enough of Karen so that I could rescue them from her. They laughed and said she was a delight and very funny.

Kerry returned, and we talked more about George and whether I could realistically escape from him. She thought that I should let the police handle the problem. I explained to her that I had already told the police, and they said it was a domestic problem which we should deal with ourselves. She stared into my eyes with such empathy that she was clearly concerned with our safety. "I would let ye stay here, Frances, but it's probably too close to George."

Yeah! he'd soon find out, Kelly, and I would be dragged out of here by the hair. I couldn't put you or my kids through that."

She took some face powder out of her bag and told me to go to the ladies and use it while she watched the kids. Looking in the mirror, I could see why she'd given me the powder: the makeup had worn off, and my bruises were showing. The powder helped to cover them, but it was not as good as the makeup I'd used earlier.

When I arrived back at the table, there were sandwiches and another drink. Kerry fed Leon his sandwich in small pieces, placing each one gently into his mouth. Karen and Deborah had no problem getting through theirs. I couldn't thank Kerry enough for her friendship: it meant so much to me.

When Kerry left to go back to her work, my mind went back into panic mode, desperate to find a way of escaping. However, I could not find clarity in my mind and felt nervous about going home. On occasions now, I was beginning to feel that I was losing all sense of reason. Unable to move forward, I tried to convince myself that if I stayed strong, I would find a way, but every day it was becoming more and more difficult. The thought of us being free from George was all that I wished for.

Just then, one of the soldiers approached me. "Excuse me, Frances. I don't want to intrude but are you okay?" he inquired. He apologised for overhearing Kelly's advice about George and expressed his disgust at how a man could treat a young woman that way.

"Is he the father of your children?" one of the other soldiers asked.

"Yeah, he is." There was a look of anger from all three of them.

"My name's Chip, and that's Bret and Steve."

"Hi, I'm Frances! Thanks for entertaining my kids."

"That's okay, but I think Karen was entertaining us," they all laughed. They pulled their chairs closer to my table, away from where the kids were playing.

"We did notice your face was bruised, but it seemed impolite to point it out. Seriously, Frances, if you want us to go and sort this bloke out, just tell us where to find him." It was hard to believe they would do that for a stranger. I declined the offer, not wanting to drag them into my problems.

"Thanks for the offer, but I must somehow find my way out of this problem. I'm not planning on hanging around any longer."

We chatted for a while, and I was glad of the company. Listening to their stories was much more pleasurable than dwelling on my problems. Steve told me that he'd joined the Army to get out of going to prison. Bret talked about how he missed his wife and baby son. Chip said he'd always wanted to be a soldier, like his father. He was used to Army life and enjoyed the training and routine. They seemed at ease socialising with civilians in the bar and were friendly and polite. I knew there were exceptions and had met soldiers under different circumstances. Maybe that was them while they were under orders on that occasion. I had lost all sense of the time and suddenly realised I needed to get the kids ready to go home. Chip helped to get the toys and books into the pram tray.

"Thanks, Chip. I appreciate ye doing that."

"You're welcome, Frances. I hope to see you back in the bar soon. That sincere offer of help is still on the table should you need it. Take care of yourself!"

The children became tired on the way home. It wouldn't take me too long to get them into a bath and prepare them for bedtime stories. This would be an early night for them and, hopefully, a peaceful evening for me. It had been a great day out, and it was just what we all needed. With any luck, I thought George wouldn't arrive back early and Nula would pop in for a chat.

By the time I finished the bedtime story, it was seven o'clock. They were all sound asleep, so I crept downstairs, made myself a cup of tea, lit a cigarette, and sat in the quiet of the kitchen. I hoped George wouldn't find out I'd been talking to the soldiers. It would have been a disastrous situation for me.

There was a knock on the kitchen window, and I could see Nula holding up a bottle of wine and a packet of cigarettes. She smiled at me, and I gestured for her to come in. We chatted about my day, and I told her about the soldiers and their offer to, "sort George out." She grinned and suggested that maybe I should let them.

"Yeah, I would be lying if I said that I hadn't thought about letting them go ahead and do it. But, I couldn't get them dragged into my problems, and they'd be in so much trouble with the Army, if they got caught. I couldn't be responsible for doing that to anyone."

Nula grabbed two glasses from the cabinet and filled them with white wine. We each lit another cigarette, and we were soon discussing my situation with George again. Nula asked if I had any more thoughts about finding a way out.

"I may have to narrow my expectations and look for somewhere closer than Belfast. It would have been nice to be close to Sinead, but it feels like that is just not going to happen. Also, if I put a claim in for benefits, they would want to know who the father of my children is, and I was worried that they would inform him of my new address. If he found out where I lived, he would turn up there every time he was drunk. That's another problem for me to sort out. The more I tried to stay positive, the more problems I would find. Despite these thoughts, I wasn't about to give up, even if I felt deflated. My faith that there would be a way out was powerful, and I could not stay in this situation any longer.

As I looked across the table at Nula, it was clear from her expression that her concern for me and the children was intense.

Although I knew we would miss being neighbours, she would be delighted for me if I could get away. We ran through various scenarios as we finished the wine and smoked cigarettes late into the evening.

I got to bed just after midnight and was asleep within minutes. In the morning, I awoke to find the girls jumping on my bed, asking if they could have their breakfast. It took a moment before I realised George had not come home. It felt great to get a good night's sleep and feel refreshed. I was relieved to have avoided any possible confrontation with him. There was no telling when he would return home, and I was delighted to get up and spend time playing with the kids. It gave me a sense of how life could be if we were free from him.

Karen and Deborah had made the most of being allowed to run around the house and make a noise. I dashed frantically around, tidying and getting myself ready for the day. I gazed out of the windows, expecting to see George coming up the road, plastered and stinking of alcohol. Finally, hoping to avoid what was to come, I got the kids washed, and dressed, then knocked for Nula to see if she wanted to walk with us.

"Yeah, Frances, just give me a minute to prepare." It was about eleven thirty when we were strolling down the road with the kids. The air was fresh, and patches of sun beamed through the clouds. It was a perfect day to be out. The prospect of running into George now was concerning, but we soon reached the park without any sight of him. Nula rushed over to the shop while I kept an eye on the kids running around happily playing while baby Leon lay sleeping in the pram.

As I waited, Paddy, George's cousin, came over and told me about the drunken mess that George had been in the previous night. "He tried to fucking fight with everyone in the pub and then out on the street, doing the old fucking Kung Fu shit," he said while trying to mimic his moves. Paddy looked very comical, and the children laughed while watching his little demonstration. Luckily, they were not aware of who he was trying to mimic.

"Do you know what happened to him after that, Paddy, because he never came home last night? Although to be honest with ye, I was relieved to get a good night's sleep."

Paddy laughed and said, "Well, ye wouldn't have wanted him home in that fucking state now. But no, I don't know where he went after that. I feel sorry for ye: it must be awful for you, having to live with that shit. I left the pub, embarrassed at him for being my cousin. People were fucking laughing at the stupid idiot."

"If ye see him along the road, don't tell him ye saw me, please, Paddy!"

"No problem, Frances. Look after yourself and the kids." As Paddy walked off, I couldn't help wondering where George had ended up.

Nula returned with lollies for the kids and cigarettes for us. We lit them up straight away, and I passed on to her what Paddy had told me. She could see I was worried now, being so out in the open. She knew George well enough by now to know that this would likely come back on me somehow. "The hotel bar will be open in half an hour. Ye could hide out there for a while, to just sort your head out. Ye don't seem up to seeing George just yet!"

Nula was right: I wasn't ready to face George. She said she would stay for a drink but then had to take Sean to meet his dad for lunch. Meanwhile, we sat smoking our cigarettes and watching the children play in the park. I'd asked them to avoid the swings now as some older rowdy children were playing in that area. Still, it was fine as they were happy enough just running about chasing after each other.

I knew I would have to face the music sooner or later, so I decided on later. Regardless of last night, I knew he would be angry with me anyway; I wouldn't have been home to make his food whenever he got in. So, I decided I might as well be in trouble for something more than that; the abuse wouldn't be any different.

At that moment, I was happy being out and watching my kids running free in the park. I loved the sound of them giggling and shouting at one another. I told myself that being out in the fresh air would do me and the kids the world of good.

I was soon up, swinging the kids around until I was dizzy, but the girls couldn't get enough and kept asking, "Again, do it again!" I obliged but eventually collapsed on the grass, laughing as everything spun around in my head.

By now, we were all ready to go to the hotel and get a drink and some crisps. Nula took the kids to our regular table, then put some songs on the jukebox while I went to the bar and got the drinks, plus some Tayto, cheese and onion crisps for all of us. Hopefully, that would keep the kids quiet while I chatted to Nula. Someone had put "Stand by Your Man" on the jukebox, forcing me to consider George and his effect on me. I disagreed with the lyrics; I didn't think that women should stand by and suffer just because they were married; that wasn't the message I wanted to send to my daughters.

Nula finished her crisps and left to have lunch with her husband. I wasn't alone for long when a girl about my age came and sat near us. She immediately took to the kids and remarked that they were making her broody. She told me that her name was Shannon, and she had no children. She had been trying but just hadn't been lucky yet.

It wasn't long before we were chatting like we had known each other for years. I liked her a lot, and we clicked straight away. She was tall and slim with long, blond, shiny hair. She was bubbly and asked if she could take Leon onto her lap. I said it would be fine with me, although I wasn't sure if he would cry. Leon seemed happy sitting with her: he was smiling a lot, and she looked so content watching him. "I hope ye get pregnant soon. You would make a great mother," I told her.

We soon discovered that we lived very close to one another. It was great to have some different conversations to distract me. We both saw that this might be a great friendship. I hadn't told her about my troubles with George. She had asked about my family, thinking that she might know them.

I explained that I had grown up in a convent and knew little about my family, although I had some first cousins who often used this bar. When I told her who they were, she said she knew them.

"So, who gives ye a wee break from the kids then, Frances, if ye have no family?"

"No one does. I've never had a break except when I was giving birth." Shannon was surprised by what I was telling her.

We continued chatting until the kids started to get bored, and I needed to get home and make them some lunch.

"It was great to meet ye, Shannon. Maybe I'll see ye again for a drink."

"Hang on, and I'll walk up the road with ye. Give ye a hand with these wee ones."

We walked along the road, Shannon pushing the pram with Deborah sitting in front. I held Karen's hand. All the while, I was hoping that George wouldn't appear suddenly from somewhere. I wouldn't know how to explain him to this new friend I'd just met. He was bound to do or say something to embarrass me in front of her and put her off. We arrived at Shannon's place first, and she kindly invited me in so the kids could have lunch with her. It was a very sweet gesture, so I accepted. The girls enjoyed cheese on toast while Leon had some tomato soup with small pieces of bread. Shannon's home was lovely, with beautiful furniture that I couldn't help but admire.

As we sipped tea and nibbled on biscuits, Shannon confided in me that she was going through a divorce. She had a boyfriend, who visited a few nights a week, but she was trying to keep the relationship under wraps until the divorce was finalised, wanting to avoid any unnecessary drama with her husband. In turn, I shared with her some of the details of my own situation and explained that I needed to be discreet about socialising with her, as my husband wouldn't react well.

"He doesn't like it when I have friends. I hope you understand what I am dealing with, Shannon."

"It's fine, Frances. I recognise that sort of relationship. What's good for him isn't good for you. Listen, if ye ever wanna talk, ye know where I am."

I was relieved to have cleared the air with Shannon. When I arrived home, I was pleased that George still hadn't returned. I assumed he must be sobering up at his mother's house, which suited me fine. I could now breathe a sigh of relief and let my guard down for a little while. He would never know I hadn't been at home waiting for him.

As the weeks passed, my relationship with George remained unchanged. I finally got a break from the constant demands of parenting when Shannon kindly offered to care for the children, insisting I take all the time I needed. Occasionally, I'd leave them at her house for several hours, granting me the luxury of uninterrupted conversations with Kelly. It was a refreshing change for all of us. The children adored Shannon. She was genuinely kind and caring, and they sensed that immediately.

I had cultivated a circle of friends at the hotel, providing me with companionship during my visits. With Shannon willing to babysit, I seized the opportunity to attend a few live music events, which proved to be a welcome diversion. Meanwhile, Nula remained a constant presence, and on pleasant days, we often ventured to the park with the kids."

Shannon was exceptionally great with my children. She once said it was great practice for when she got pregnant and had her own children to look after. She knew I wasn't too far away should she need me, but so far, she never had.

On one of my trips to the hotel, I met Veronica, who lived in the Army camp in married quarters. She was about my age but bigger than me, around five feet tall, and had short brown hair. I thought she had been a bit of a tomboy growing up because she still looked like one. When we met, I was at the bar with Karen, who was bugging me for more fizzy drinks. Knowing she had already finished her second one, I told her that she'd had enough for now. Otherwise, she'd want to go to the toilet on the way home.

Veronica overheard our conversation and offered the coke left in the bottle she had used to mix her drink. Karen thanked her and smiled now that she had got her way. She asked if Karen was my little sister, and I answered, "No, she's my daughter."

"But she called ye Frances, and ye don't look old enough to have a daughter that age." I thanked her for the compliment and told her I had another two children. We chatted, and so we started a long friendship.

Veronica knew someone who worked in the guardroom and got me a visitor's pass for when I wanted to get into the camp to see her. She had a couple of kids, a boy and a girl, and I instantly became fond of them. I soon made her aware of my dilemma with George.

George was furious when I finally got the courage to inform him about my leaving a letter with Mr McConnell. He believed what I was saying, and it had some effect. He was now careful not to punch me where it would be easily noticed. Also, he was out of the house more often than before. However, his drinking was as bad as ever and when he eventually remembered where he lived, he still relied on me to help getting him in and up to his bed. He had always been argumentative and ready to kick and punch me when he was drunk and sometimes forgot about the letter.

One night, he punched me so hard in the stomach that I collapsed onto the kitchen floor. I cried out for him to stop, and then he kicked me as hard as he could in my back several times. The pain surged through my body, and I couldn't catch my breath to speak. I braced myself for whatever else would follow a few more kicks and a lot of verbal abuse.

I'd been used to abuse my whole life, with the nuns at the convent and now with him. I lay there listening while he complained that his shoe had busted while he was kicking me. He sounded like it was my fault for making him do that to me. Meanwhile, Karen had crept downstairs and wandered into the kitchen to see what all the commotion was about. She had witnessed some of it and was crying for her daddy to stop it. For the next few weeks, I walked around in excruciating pain.

After that day, Karen would readily tell people that her dad had broken his shoe, kicking Frances. I would tell her that people didn't need to know about that, but it didn't stop her. She grew increasingly clingy to me, not wanting me to leave her sight and hoping to protect me. Knowing that my children would grow up affected was the last straw.

One morning, when I was feeling a little better, I used my visitor pass to get into the Army camp with my children. It was a beautiful sunny day in July, and we were visiting Veronica so the kids could all play together. There was a play park opposite her house, and there never appeared to be any other kids playing in it. It felt like a safe space for us.

We had a brilliant time eating sandwiches, pushing the kids on the swings, and listening to the music on the radio. Veronica and I shared so many stories of our lives. She was divorced and would soon have to leave the Army married quarters. She was just waiting to be allocated a council house in Antrim, where her two sisters lived. The council had already told her it would be ready in a few months. I was dreading her leaving, but I knew it would be great for her.

When it came time to go home, there was more than a hint of sadness. The kids didn't want to leave, but we had to go.

"Are ye goanna be all right going back home, Frances? Why don't ye all stay here?"

"I couldn't. It would be lovely, but George would go mad when I returned home!"

"No, Frances, why don't you stay for good? You and the kids. We will make do with sleeping arrangements and everything else. Then you can come to Antrim with us, and we can help each other. What do ye think? It might be the answer for the both of us."

I was astounded. It was a lot to take in, but I immediately knew I had to say yes. I'd been trying to get away from George for ages, so there was no way I could look a gift horse in the mouth, and anyway, I wanted to do it.

"Are ye sure ye want to do this, Veronica? I mean, I would love to make that work. If we wouldn't get on each other's nerves, then I think, yes."

I couldn't believe it; this might be the solution we both needed. I found out that day that Veronica had gone through the same thing with her husband. When he was off duty and drunk, he would beat her up. I felt we had a lot in common. Also, we got on very well, loved each other's kids and could help each other through it.

After I accepted her offer, I quickly returned home, leaving the children with her, and I got clothes, nappies, and anything I could carry back to her house.

We moved in with Veronica that night. I got the kids sorted and they were soon sound asleep. Then, we sat up and had a few lagers from the fridge to celebrate a new chapter in our friendship.

At last, I felt at peace in a way I had not known since I'd lived at McConnell's house. George would not be able to get to me here; the Army would keep him out.

The next few months were very busy. With just a few months to go until we had to move out, there was much to be done to get the house ready to hand back to the Army. Fortunately, although I'd received no formal education in the convent, the one thing I had learnt to do well was clean and scrub. Without George to worry about, the work was a joy, and soon, all that was left to do was pack up all our possessions ready for the move.

Veronica and I quickly fell into a routine, and our children formed an inseparable bond. Despite the crowded quarters, with prams and bags of clothes strewn about, we functioned as a team, finding solace in each other's company as we navigated through life's challenges. While the security of the base provided a sense of safety, adjusting to George's absence and finding true peace took time.

Anticipation bubbled within us as we eagerly awaited moving day. Fifty miles from Omagh, Antrim represented a fresh start, free from the shadow of George and his family. The prospect of newfound freedom filled us with excitement. No longer constrained by fear of scrutiny or judgement, we envisioned a future brimming with possibilities in our new home. For the first time in a long while, thoughts of the future filled me with hope and optimism. All I desired was a life filled with joy, contentment, and happiness for my children and me.

Epilogue

I wish I could tell you that everything turned out wonderfully and that we lived happily ever after once I was free from George's grasp. But real life rarely unfolds so neatly. Happily-ever-afters are more at home in fairy tales, and I still had plenty of challenges ahead of me. Despite everything I had endured, I wasn't prepared for what lay ahead.

Tragically, George soon caught up with me and the children and snatched them away from me. It shattered my heart; the pain was unbearable. He cast me aside, cruelly informing me that I'd never see my kids again. His actions were driven by a desire to hurt and punish me for leaving; he had previously paid little attention to the children. I later learned from a neighbour that he had moved them in with his mother, leaving her to care for them. I felt utterly adrift, paralysed by fear, unsure how to go on without my children by my side.

I found myself embroiled in a relentless cycle of court appearances, but it soon became painfully apparent that the judge favoured my in-laws' side. To make matters worse, the judge was a close friend of George's father, and their shared outings, such as fishing trips, were openly referred to in court. Each time George appeared in court, he was accompanied by his family, who spun elaborate tales that were riddled with falsehoods.

Regrettably, I lacked the support of my own family in court, and there was no one to advocate for me or speak on my behalf. My upbringing in an orphanage worked against me in court. In Ireland, familial ties carry significant weight, and one's background is often scrutinised through the lens of family connections. A social worker underscored this point, suggesting to the judge that because my mother had abandoned me, there was a high likelihood that I, too, would abandon my children.

As those hurtful words rang out in the courtroom, tears welled up in my eyes, and I felt a surge of anger pulse through me. The mere thought of willingly leaving my children was unfathomable to me.

The judge left no room for doubt; without a home of my own to offer the children, gaining custody seemed an insurmountable challenge. Even though the house my friend and I shared with her two young children provided more space than the cramped conditions at

George's mother's residence, my pleas fell on deaf ears. If I was to have a chance of having the children with me, I needed to have a home of my own first.

Turning to the council for assistance only compounded my frustration. No matter how fervently I argued, my voice seemed drowned out by the bureaucracy. They maintained that housing assistance couldn't be granted until I had custody of the children. Thus, a frustrating cycle ensued, with no clear path forward. Eventually, the judge ruled that disrupting the children's routine by relocating them was now out of the question. While I was permitted visitation rights, the terms were strictly dictated by George.

Every weekend, my friend would get her sister to babysit her children and we would thumb a lift from Antrim to Omagh as we couldn't afford the fair. It was fifty-five miles and took well over an hour by car. George was always aware I was coming, but when I arrived he often decided not to let me see the children. I remember seeing Karen at the window crying because she wanted to see me. Once, she ran out to the front door shouting Mammy, but her dad grabbed her arm and my friend and I watched on angrily as George pulled her shorts down and slapped her hard for crying and trying to get to me. I heard her sobbing, and at that moment, I wanted him to suffer the way he was making our daughter suffer.

I could have tried going back to court, but it was clear that I wouldn't get anywhere. I carried on trying to see the children until eventually, I had to make the heart breaking decision, regardless of the cost to myself, to leave them with their father. To have carried on would have caused even more distress, especially to Karen, and I couldn't bear to witness their continued suffering.

Some years after leaving George, I divorced and married my second husband, Kevin, whom I met while he was serving in the Royal Air Force in Northern Ireland. We had two sons, Darren and Christopher. I have a very close relationship with them and am immensely proud of the people they have become. I currently live with my son Darren and his son, Kieran, whom I've raised as my own.

For many years I had no contact at all with my three oldest children. When I did finally meet with the girls again, as teenagers, I found out that they had been told that I was dead! Needless to say, it was difficult for all of us. Shortly after this, Deborah came to England to live with us for several years; while Karen relocated just a few miles away from our home. It was great to have this time with them but unfortunately, it didn't last.

I met up with Leon while I was over in Belfast campaigning for an inquiry into the abuse suffered by children in convents in Northern Ireland. Our initial meeting lasted just for a few hours and it was amazing. However, it was telling that, although he was in his thirties, he told me that he had gotten, "The green light," from Daddy before speaking to me.

We met again, several times, when I had the joy of meeting his beautiful children and he finally met up with his two younger half-brothers. During one of our visits, George spoke with Leon and expressing his remorse for depriving him of a relationship with me. He also told Leon that, I had done nothing wrong.

The years spent in the convent and my tumultuous relationship with George profoundly affected me. For many years, I felt broken, incomplete and worthless. However, after some challenging times and with support, from family, friends and others, I have finally ended up in a place where I am content and have accepted how my life has turned out. I have no anger left in me. Now, I try not to look back but to keep moving forward.

Frances Reilly 2024

Printed in Great Britain
by Amazon